Mysteries on the Mountain

Mysteries on the Mountain

A Collection of Summit Hill History, Ghost Stories and Lore

David A. Wargo

Dedication

This book is dedicated to my sweetheart, my wife and my best friend, Katie. She has indulged my interest, joined in my passion and has been there for me in one of the most difficult parts of my life. This revised volume is also dedicated to my wonderful daughter, Kathryn who is smart and wants to learn about everything. Never stop learning, my dear.

Special thanks also go to my parents, Bernie and Darlene for their support; my brother, Jeff who awakened my fascination and interest in ghosts; Bob Vybrenner, who shared my interest in local folklore, encouraged me to record the stories and contributed to this book and all of the folks in the Summit Hill Historical Society who have generously supported my efforts and helped me stage a worthwhile event and to all of you who helped me find this material. Thank you all so much.

Notes on Stories

All of the stories except where noted are true in the sense that they are folklore that has been handed down from generation to generation. We offer them at face value for what they are worth.

Several of the stories have been verified using multiple sources. Except where stated all sources are and will remain confidential. The author personally has experienced some of the tales related here and it is noted in those stories.

Only stories penned by the author have been rewritten in this volume.

The bonus story about Edmund Brennan was penned as a treat for the first ghost tour and is a work of fiction.

The pictures except where noted on the rear of the title page are royalty free clipart or photographs owned by the author.

We are looking for more oral history of the town and in the Panther Valley. Your name will be kept strictly confidential.

Forward

It has been nineteen years since I self-published the first edition of this collection of ghost stories from Summit Hill and in that time I have had a great deal of experiences to add to my background in the paranormal. Some views have refined themselves and others have changed but the one thing that remains the same is I do believe there is life beyond death. It is not the same as the physical life we live here and now but I genuinely believe our conscience and our intelligence may survive beyond the grave.

The stories contained in this book have been documented and told exactly how they were related to me by area residents who personally experienced them or by my own personal experiences. Most stories have a postscript following it that details the historical background, my research notes and other information that is as factual as I can find. There are end notes and a short biography to support the historical nature of the volume. I have curated and documented these stories as thoroughly as I can so that the volume you now have can serve not only as a group of ghost stories but snapshots of anecdotal history about our town.

I have done my best to document their experiences and anecdotes, but in the end the tales in this book are oral history at best and stand for better or for worse on their own. Take them for what they are worth.

My purpose for capturing them is to ensure they continue to be told even after we have all leave this mortal coil. So please enjoy them.

Forward from Historical Society Manuscript

This is my first collection of folklore compiled and researched on my own for the purposes of preserving the oral history of the Panther Valley area. I have been conducting this research for four years now, and I am pleased to share with you this set of tales about the darker side of Summit Hill. Whether you believe in ghosts and spirits or not, folklore and oral tradition is a rich part of any culture. We lose so much as our older folks die and leave this earthly plane of existence. Much of our oral history has been lost in the dust of the cemeteries in this area, but some still survives. This is the first in a series of volumes to record and track this history. Some of these tales which I researched had been previously published in a tome called the Specters of Summit Hill written with a writing partner Rebecca Rayder Venable. I have rewritten and updated them here so that you know the most up-to-date information on each one. Collecting oral history never stops and this is the first of what I hope to be several volumes of compiled folklore for this area.

David Wargo

July 4, 2002

Table of Contents

Do You Believe in Ghosts?

This is one of the loaded questions that seems to occur throughout the course of every relationship between two people at some point in their lives. "Do you believe in ghosts?" It is a fair question that can be used to judge the openness of people to new beliefs or ideas that may not easily be believed or explained. I can tell you that I went through phases where I was not sure, to definitely not believing, to not caring and finally to the place where I am today. If you ask me this question, I will tell you that I do believe in the possibility of ghosts.

I have had some strange experiences in my life that cannot be easily explained or rationally dismissed. I have seen lights turn off without a human hand and heard disembodied voices call my name. I have even seen a shadow that was not cast by a person stand and observe me. You ask me if I believe in ghosts, and I will tell you that they are possible. All of these things mentioned could be explained rationally. A faulty circuit in the case of the light, an overactive imagination in the case of the voices and possibly a hallucination or a dream in the last case; these explanations could make everything fit nice and neat into the world we know, but unfortunately life is not always that black and white. It is said that there are many shades of gray in our lives.

In the case of the phenomena described, I can offer the following facts: the electricity was fine and the switch was working perfectly; I was awake and alone when I heard my name called—and event which occurred several times in my life; the shadow was seen by other people in my family as I found out several years later. Do I believe in ghosts? Yes, I do have theories about what ghosts could be, if they exist. I will share these in a later essay

Right now though, I would like to offer my beliefs on ghosts. First, I believe there are several types of ghosts and related phenomena that appear to living people. Second, I believe that depending on the activity level of the ghost, anyone may be able to have an encounter with a phantom. Even so, I believe that there are people who are susceptible to finding more passive spirits which do not normally interact with living humans. We would refer to those persons as psychic. Third, I believe in God and Satan and that some ghosts may be demonic in nature but camouflaged under the guise of being a helpless spirit. Their purpose is to deceive and destroy.

There are also things in which I do not believe. First, I do not believe that there is anyone incapable of encountering the supernatural; it's just that some of us are not as sensitive to our natural world as others might be. I tend to fall into this category. Second, I do not believe that there is anyone on this planet who can communicate at will with spirits. If spirits are people, then they also have the ability to refuse to communicate and some so-called channeler will not always successfully communicate with ghosts at will and upon demand. I believe that there are people who can communicate with spirits, but only if the spirit desires the communication. It's like a telephone: you cannot be forced to answer your phone or talk to a neighbor when living so where is the logic in being forced to when you are deceased? Finally, I think that all of us at some point have experienced something unusual and not easily explained. Note that this does not mean ghosts, but have you ever felt an urge to do something that you would not normally do or to not do something you usually do? Later, your urge turns out to have protected you. Depending on the circumstances, this could be almost as unnatural as a roaming ghost.

We cannot hope to explain everything, and what follows are some stories that defy simple explanation yet have been documented and experienced by people which I have met or places where I have been. As incredible as they seem, all of these stories have occurred to people with whom I am personally acquainted and have corroborated with the exception of one small tale. See if you can figure out by the end of this book which tale that might be. I will tip my hand at the end of this volume. You can consider it a contest of the mind so to speak.

Now that my beliefs are out of the way, get a warm glass of milk, turn down the lights and let us explore the hidden history of Summit Hill. On second thought, you might want to keep the lights on.

David Wargo

September 30, 2000

CHAPTER ONE

Cemetery Stories

Nestled on a mountain on the southern edge of the Pocono Mountains is the hilltop community of Summit Hill. From a small patch town in the 1820's, the town blossomed and is considered by some scholars to be the birthplace of the Industrial Revolution in America. As a result of a discovery of the purest vein of anthracite coal in the world by local miller Philip Ginter, industrialists and visionaries Josiah White and Erskine Hazard traveled to this "wilderness" north of Philadelphia to mine that coal for profit. By the mid 1800's, patch towns were established throughout the region with the area of Mauch Chunk Township situated on top of Mount Pisgah being one of those communities.

In 1889, that little community was formally incorporated into the Borough of Summit Hill and while the mines were in operation, the borough was a bustling place featuring hotels, a movie theater, two supermarkets, several stores and all the amenities of a robust mining town. To the east of the borough was a unique area that became organized as cemeteries. Due to the rest of the Panther Valley being undermined to retrieve those precious black diamonds, the only location in the area to bury people was on the eastern edge of the borough.

As a result of this unique placement there are eight cemeteries, seven of which belong to churches in the Panther Valley while the eighth is one of the few public cemeteries in Carbon County. There are over ten to twelve thousand people collectively buried in this area and at the time I am writing this that corresponds to four deceased souls for every living person in Summit Hill.

Besides these eight cemeteries along the eastern end of the town, there are two other locations in the borough that also contained cemeteries but have been now repurposed for other uses. The Old Presbyterian cemetery which was one of the oldest community cemeteries run by its namesake church is now a community park across the street from the Post Office. It was closed and converted in the early 1970's after having been overgrown and unmaintained for several years. While that is so, there are still two graves marked in this cemetery--one being mine superintendent Morgan Powell and the other being an unknown soldier that was found in a well. The other cemetery is now a garden behind St. Joseph's cemetery. It contains the remains of the two infamous Molly Maguires, Alec Campbell and Thomas Fisher. The cemetery was converted in the early 2000's, but a road tour marker still marks the location.

When we began looking for folklore to relate for our first ghost tour, our inquiries were richly rewarded with many stories, several of which deal with these cemeteries so it is only fitting to begin our journey into the paranormal in this unofficial area landmark. There are two former cemeteries with some interesting tales while three other cemeteries among the eight which remain have disclosed fascinating stories that really raise some questions about what may survive beyond the grave.

The Woman In White of Summit Hill

At the eastern edge of Summit Hill nestled in among the cemeteries is one cemetery that may share more than peace and tranquility. As you approach it especially in the evening, you may feel the cool evening breeze on your face as you gaze at its picturesque appearance. It is one of the less inhabited cemeteries as its members belong to one of the former smaller churches in town. It has an old fashioned stone wall encircling its residents with two steel gates at either end. A dirt road surrounds the cemetery which provides access to the home behind it and to the Jefferson Plane about one quarter mile back in the forest which borders two sides of the graveyard.

Inside of the wall, the cemetery is divided into four quadrants with a moss-covered road bisecting the walls. The north-south road connects the two steel gates for the purpose of providing access to hearses for funerals. The northern gate also has a smaller companion entrance for people to enter and exit its walls. The east-west road is identical in width and is somewhat curious as it runs directly into the wall. It was designed, one would imagine, to provide easier access to graves further back from the other road. The northern end does not contain very many trees, but starting from just before the intersection to the southern gate, large shade trees line the moss-covered roads creating a serene, shady roof of natural leaves for any visitors.

There are some unusual things about this resting place which seem more interesting than the landscaping. Most noticeable, the cemetery is by no means full, yet there is one grave located in the extreme southwest corner almost against the wall and a good thirty to forty feet away from the closest grave. It is a single plot with the name of a boy who apparently passed on when he was only twelve years old. The focus of activity in this cemetery appears to be around the boy, and his frequent visitor, the woman in white.

The boy was a drowning victim in the early 1930's. Many of the young men in the Panther Valley relieved the heat of summer by swimming in the local lakes and swimming holes such as the spring cistern which provided water for powering the steam engine at the engine house on the Jefferson Plane. This young man drowned while attempting to swim across the Lake Hauto dam according to some of the older residents who knew the family. As preparations were being made with the church for his funeral, a falling out allegedly occurred between the boy's father and the priest. As a result, the father buried his son not in the Orthodox cemetery- a place where his siblings are interred located next to the Polish cemetery- but he arranged for the boy to be interred in the Polish cemetery instead. Unfortunately, this young man was not the only sibling to meet an untimely fate. His sister and brother both perished in their youth also, but the sister at least was interred back in the Russian Orthodox cemetery. As the sands of time dribbled down, the boy ended up alone in the Polish cemetery. Or is he?

There is a legend according to some of the residents that on certain evenings of the month around the full moon, a woman in white can be seen roaming through the cemetery. Some folks even claim she may leave the cemetery after the witching hour and begin heading into town, but most sightings have been in the cemetery. The basic account is she materializes near the northern edge of the cemetery, walks along the road then crosses over to the little boy's grave and stands vigil over it.

Several people have separately described feeling cold in and around that corner of the cemetery. Even on the warmest summer days, you can feel cold breezes in the area there. I have seen ribbons on the cross adorning the grave move dramatically in the still of the morning air when there was not even a slight breeze, and have felt the coldness on the back of my neck. There is a spot at the intersection of the roads near a bush where you also feel strange and sometimes cold . You get the feeling you are being watched as you tarry within its stone wall perimeter.

One evening many years ago, two girls wanted to check out this legend for themselves and arrived at the cemetery just around dusk. As they eagerly scanned the cemetery looking for the mysterious specter, they got more of a thrill than they probably wanted. In the corner of the cemetery was the woman in white keeping vigil over the boy's grave. She was tall and featureless almost defying description and looked almost normal with the exception of being partially translucent. The girl who related this story to me said she could feel the hair rise on the back of her neck and both felt terror as they witnessed the ghost. They quickly and quietly backed away from the cemetery and ran back to town.

If this wasn't enough to actually believe she is there, a long-time patrolman in town has reported seeing her in the middle of the cemetery late at night. She was shrouded and emitted an unearthly glow. When questioned further, he said it was definitely human in form, but he was unable to see her face or determine what she may have been doing in the center of the cemetery, but she was facing the corner grave.

Who is she and why is she there guarding or mourning that one grave? Is it possible that she is the boy's mother or sister comforting and keeping him? If you would like to find out perhaps you could see her yourself in the evenings just after dusk as she visits the lone child in the corner of the stone-walled cemetery.

This is an artist's depiction of the Lady in White that supposedly haunts the Polish National Cemetery in the eastern end of the community.

Postscript

We conducted an investigation of this cemetery on June 28, 2002 and received a most pleasant surprise yet one we did not expect as far as location according to the legends. During our study, the temperature dropped about five to seven degrees in one spot in the northeast quadrant. Quickly we snapped the photograph seen in this photograph. The circled object is apparently an orb found over the grave of a fallen veteran from World War II.

Possible orb in motion in Polish National Cemetery (Summer 2001)

While I have reviewed this photo several times and in different ways and cannot conclusively determine whether it is really what it appeared at the time, something more striking occurred that makes the orblike object minor in comparison.

Suspicious of what could have created this anomalous photo including reflections and bugs, I returned to the cemetery in early July 2002 with my wife Katie and my ghost hunting friend and fellow historian, Bob Vybrenner. It was early evening and the sun was low in the sky. As we roamed the cemetery, I returned to the area of the above photograph and inspected the site looking for anything reflective. As I snapped photos from several different angles working my way around the spot pictured above, I felt a strong sensation like I was being watched from the cemetery wall. In my mind, I sensed the presence of an older woman dressed in a gray striped dress with a black sweater. She was very plain and older in appearance. It occurred to me she was dressed like a nun. She was quite upset with us being in the cemetery. Within a minute or two of this experience, my chest started to tighten and I felt the air get really heavy around me.

I called over to Bob and Katie and said, "I have to leave the cemetery right now. I think you both should come with me." They looked at me quizzically, but then followed me from the cemetery as I quickly walked directly for the gate. We just kept walking for about a block until the heaviness lifted and I felt normal again.

Bob asked if I was okay. I said that I was. He said, "You know, you looked a little odd, but even before you asked us to leave, I heard a woman's voice in my ear barking the order, 'Iść! Iść!' Do you know what that means?"

I had to admit I was unaware of those words. Bob said, "Those words mean 'Go! Go!' in Polish. The woman who spoke them in my ear wanted us to leave the cemetery, and then not more than a second or two later you said we had to leave."

Are Orbs Ghosts?

Digital cameras have created this orb phenomena due to the ability to create scores of photos quickly using digital technologies which can filter and interpret the visual information captured by the photographic array. Dust, dirt, bugs, rain and pollen all become major culprits in the orb phenomena. Almost every orb photograph including the one cited here probably is one of these culprits.

So can an orb be something else? While 99.9% of photographs can be explained, it is interesting to note that spirits have been portrayed as orbs in the hieroglyphics in the Egyptian tombs. In the October 2002 issue of National Geographic a photo essay shows this and explains what the orbs painted in the drawings are representing. (Williams, 2002)

Even mathematically it makes sense that cohesive energy could assume a spherical shape since it is the most efficient way to form (ie like raindrops). This is because a sphere contains the minimum or most efficient surface area of any shape to contain its volume. So if spirit energy would travel it could be spherical, but alas almost all photos are not spirits but normal substances.

We decided at that point not to return to the cemetery for a while to leave the energy settle. The three of us gathered in a circle and said a binding prayer before we left the area. I returned several times since then over the years, but the experience has not repeated itself.

The Late Night Encounter

Our town was one in which people could walk the streets without fear any time of the day or night. In fact, it was typical for people to leave their doors unlocked at night when they went to bed since violent crime was something that happened elsewhere. Even as a child growing up, I was used to such feelings of security and was never frightened to be out after dark. There is one place though people usually avoided after dark—the cemeteries at the edge of town.

At one time, Summit Hill boasted in excess of four thousand people working the mines and raising their families. The western end of town contained rich veins of coal directly underneath the top soil which is one of the reasons that one of the first viable coal companies established itself in this area. The eastern end of town was one of the few places in Panther Valley that was dirt directly over bedrock. This is where the churches and the Grand Army of the Republic decided to locate its cemeteries for the citizens. Over the years, many of Summit Hill's residents have rested eternally on the peak of the mountain catching the warm rays of the morning sun. There are so many there now that they outnumber the living almost four to one.

There were other cemeteries located in town—one behind St. Joseph's Church and one at Chestnut and Hazard. The former was for the parish congregation members while the latter contained folks from the Presbyterian parish, but most of the other churches' members are buried on the east end. Both cemeteries are now parks and while some of the occupants are still buried in those locations, many were moved into the existing cemeteries.

It is not uncommon for the police to find people mourning recent family members out in the cemeteries at night, even well after dark. Once in a while a person might spend the night at the graveside of the recently departed. It wasn't uncommon for teenagers to drive out to the end of the street and park near the cemeteries to attend drinking parties off the dirt road in the woods behind the graveyards. For that reason, the police patrolled out there at night especially on weekends. Even this normal expectation did not prepare a particular patrolman for the encounter they experienced one evening about twenty years ago.

It was two or three o'clock in the morning when a senior patrolman and his trainee decided to ride out White Street and circle the block to return on Ludlow

Street and head back into town. At that time of night, most of White Street in the region of the cemeteries is dark and heavily shadowed. There is a streetlamp at the edge of the cemeteries, one about halfway up the cemetery and then one at the corner; all three on the southern side of the street. The northern side of the street has no light and starting at the GAR cemetery, there are trees lining that side of the street to the end of the block. In the shadows of the other side of the street, they could see a lone figure walking toward the end of the cemeteries. At the point they saw him, he had just reached the first of the trees planted outside the GAR cemetery. He was in shadows, so it was difficult to make him out, and because of this and the fact that he was out at such a late time, they decided to get more information. As they pulled closer, they could see that it was a man, but they were unable to make out any details as far as his face or even a description of what exactly he was wearing. He walked at a steady pace and did not acknowledge the officers beside him, so the senior patrolman who was driving the car rolled down his window and yelled, "Hey buddy!"

The figure did not answer him and just kept his steady treading up the street, so the officer repeated himself. "Hey! I'm talking to you! Where do you think you're goin'?"

Again there was no response from the figure who was now nearing the upper gate at the end of the block. The rookie partner said that the longer this attempted questioning went on, the more uneasy he felt, and almost subconsciously he felt the hair on the back of his neck begin to tingle. The senior partner was a gruff person, but he too was beginning to get bad feelings about this encounter so they decided that they would just follow this person and hope for an opportunity to stop him as he reached the end of the block.

The figure continued to approach the upper gate near the garage at a steady pace and without faltering at the gate, he turned into the cemetery and started to walk down the road just inside the gate. Seizing upon this opportunity, the patrolman quickly reached the gate, swerved the car's front end in so that the headlights shined on the road and the driver switched on the high beams. This simple action did nothing to prepare them for the shock they received when they realized that there was no one in the cemetery! The beams cut through the inky darkness to reveal an empty road from the gate to the woods. No one within the range of the headlights was visible. Their stranger had walked into the graveyard and just dissolved into the night leaving two very troubled officers behind.

Postscript

The stories in this volume formed the basis of the ghost tours conducted by the Summit Hill Historical Society in the early 2000's. We ran that tour for five years and in that time held several special bonus events along with the tour including readings from Poe, an Irish Wake, a recreation of a 19th century interment service and more. One of the final years, the members of the Panther Valley Paranormal Society which was an organization headed by my then partner Jerry Matika and myself, conducted a paranormal investigation in the cemetery during the tour. When we reached the cemetery, Jerry would describe how an investigation was conducted, the tools used and answered questions.

The final tour happened to be lighted by the full moon. It was around midnight and after the question and answer session the group returned to their cars to head to the museum for refreshments. As I turned to leave the location, Jerry asked me to wait because he had something to tell me.

I asked him what was going on. He told me that his son was in the middle of the cemetery with equipment when he happened to look up to see a man in a dark suit walking between the stones in the center section of the cemetery several feet from his location. He was momentarily surprised to see the figure that seemed to walk fairly quickly through the uneven property, a feat quite difficult for almost anyone due to the ruts. He shadowed him from a distance as the figure headed northeast through the section toward the road along the garage. When he reached the road the figure turned north and started walking down the road toward the woods. Surprisingly, as the young man watched, the figure dissolved into the air as it neared the fence leaving behind an apprehensive and startled investigator.

I asked Jerry if his son could provide details about the figure and he said because of the full moon the teen was able to describe him in detail. Intrigued I wrote down the description and compared it later that night to my notes. They seemed to match in detail, height, build, dress, and style, all which were visible in the bright light of the full moon. Next, to be certain there was no discrepancies, I returned to the original patrolman who first told me the story. I asked him to describe the man again. When he did, I showed him the notes I made from the tale Jerry's son related. The color faded from his face as the police officer told me the description in my notes matched his memory of the man from so many years ago.

When I told him who the young man was, he told me he had not told that story to anyone before I asked him four years previously, so no one to his knowledge would have had a description as detailed as the one he gave me. In fact, he also said that even when he tells the story the details of the figure were not usually related, leaving us with the mystery as to why the man reappeared so many years later and the question as to how often he has really been seen by others.

The Most Haunted Cemetery in Summit Hill

Main Entrance, Grand Army Cemetery, Summit Hill PA

The Grand Army of the Republic Cemetery is located at the eastern end of Hazard and White Streets occupying twelve acres just beyond St. Joseph's Cemetery and before St. John's Slovak Lutheran Cemetery. It is the cemetery in which a late night visitor[1] sent chills down the spines of a few local police officers. Those two men on that late night so many years ago were not the only ones to have been frightened or at the very least to have their senses tested by this magnificent cemetery. Several people reported their own experiences related to this landmark property.

A local caretaker told this story. He and his young helper were trimming weeds one humid July evening. It was dusk and the humidity created a mist which rolled into the cemetery quickly filling the air with a milky haze making it difficult to see anything. The older man was near White Street trimming the grass along the fence while the young man was in the center section along the north road. From his position the older man was able to observe all of the gates and entry points into the cemetery from the street. A gate on the rear of the cemetery was blocked by a large pile of debris to keep people from entering along the dirt road where a gate once was.

As the young man worked, he began to pick up snatches of conversation through the fog from people walking within the property. He figured they had come to visit some of their deceased friends and relatives and continued his work. The figures moved in the mist near him and he stopped again and listened. To his surprise, the figures seemed to be discussing news from several years ago as if it was happening that day which seemed odd to him. He left his location to find the caretaker to see if he knew who the people were. When he found the caretaker, he related what he heard from the visitors to the older man. The boss seemed surprised and responded to his helper that while he was along the fence no one entered or left the cemetery. They were there when the fog began to obscure the cemetery so both of them knew there had been no one inside when they started working. The boy felt very uneasy, but finally both men got the nerve to search the fog covered cemetery. By that time, the figures were gone leaving only the mysterious conversation and encounter in the fog behind.

The cemeteries are not only a prime spot for the dead to live, but on weekends and summer nights, the woods past the burial grounds are a prime hangout for teenagers and young adults partying away the evenings and weekends. Because of the seclusion, it also has been a location for late night trysts. As such, it is not unusual for the police to sit out there at night to discourage these human night visitors. Once in a while however these police guardians find themselves under the scrutiny of some unusual sentries. Several times in the past few years, police officers out on patrol who have sat at the top of White Street late at night have felt a distinct rapping on the back of the car in the middle of the night. A few of them even investigated it by searching the rear of the vehicle but to date, no one has found any explanation for the tapping. It would be easy to dismiss this as a tree branch hitting the window from a late night breeze common on the summit, but the problem with this explanation is the vehicle is never near enough to the trees when the rapping occurs.

Some officers have described a different phenomenon besides the rapping occurring late at night within the cemetery. More than one person has told me while they were sitting in their car observing the area or doing paperwork, they would hear a solo bugler playing "Taps" coming from somewhere near the center of the cemetery. While no one is seen in the cemetery, those mournful solitary notes will continue on the breeze until they fade into the night or the song ends. While no one describes being scared by the music, it did intrigue them that these notes from the past continue to play in the present.

Another older gentleman recalled an incident from his youth. He skipped school one afternoon and headed to the cemetery to collect discarded vegetables from the landfill there for the purpose of feeding his rabbits. He found some lettuce and carrots at the landfill and headed home to feed his pets when he encountered an apparition of a man in a long dark coat, dark hat with a brim and white shirt who motioned to him to come near the shed. Terrified the boy ran home without looking back. This anecdote would be isolated if it wasn't for the story of the late-night visitor which related a similar figure entering the cemetery in the middle of the night.

The most interesting anecdote about this cemetery was from a website called the Shadowlands[2]. The story describes a headless miner that appears in the winter and the springtime roaming the Grand Army cemetery. One officer I interviewed encountered the specter one February night during an ice storm. As he described it, he was patrolling White Street near the cemetery and saw a figure standing out in the middle of the upper section. As he observed it, he noticed an eerie red glow surrounding it. The police officer said the figure appeared to have no head above the shoulders of his cloaked body. He decided that whatever it was should not be disturbed and quickly retreated back to the town.

The story would end here if it weren't for his curiosity to determine what he really witnessed. When the sun rose in the morning, he returned to the site of the specter and learned the true nature of the fearful apparition. To his amazement and relief, the apparition turned out to be a burlap covered propane tank attached to a burner that outlined the perimeter of the grave. Caretakers used the device when the ground was frozen to thaw it enough to open the grave. At night the propane burners would glow red from the flames burning within the tubes. With the growing availability of backhoes, I believe these devices aren't used extensively anymore.

It is ironic that this tale which could be considered quite spooky is one that we can explain or can we? Perhaps a specter does roam—a miner in search of a discarded head. Or maybe there is a mystical portal in the center of the property that can transport sights and sounds of the past into the present to be re-experienced. The possibilities are fascinating if one is open to the world beyond the physical.

Postscript

The incident described by the police officers I interviewed practically begged to be tested. So over the course of a few evenings in 2004, my wife Katie and I decided to see if we could duplicate and optimally find an explanation for the car rapping experiences described by various police officers. The first test was on a Monday evening in mid-May 2004 around 9PM. We drove to the upper gate of the GAR cemetery and turned around facing toward town and parked there near the gate. There was open space all around us and we were at least fifteen feet from the fence which was separated from the road by a grassy shoulder. The cemetery had trees and brush east of us about sixty feet away so the immediate location was exposed and easy to observe from the mirrors of the car. There was a gentle breeze that evening and we waited for about twenty minutes but nothing out of the ordinary occurred.

We decided to try again a few evenings after that night. Once again we returned to the spot we parked at the last time we experimented, and the clear evening made everything easy to watch. Unlike the first night though, this evening was much more humid and as it cooled the moisture began to accumulate on the car body. As we sat and observed the area around us, we were startled by two hard raps on the rear left side of the car that shook the car not up and down but sideways. When the raps occurred, I first shot glances at the mirrors but saw nothing near the car. I immediately jumped out of the car to see if I could spot anyone running from the area with a flashlight, but there was no one to be found. Even stranger than the rapping though were the marks on the left rear bumper. As I looked at the dew, my mind raced because there in front of me on the left side of the bumper was a handprint in the dew.

We went home shortly after that but returned a few more evenings over the next couple weeks although that experience never repeated itself. I was left with more questions than answers since; unlike the police we were purposely waiting and watching for someone to sneak up on the car. The other unusual observation was that it took a violent hit to make the car move sideways like it did. There was no wind that night and even if there was, it would not explain the handprint. While it is possible someone did sneak up on us, they would have had to disappear within the two seconds it took for me to jump out of the car with a light and what makes that even more unlikely is the closest cover was at least fifty to sixty feet away. There would have been nowhere for anyone to hide.

We have returned several times since that spring evening, but the experience has to date not recurred.

With regard to the phantom Taps player and the other noises that people report hearing not only in the GAR cemetery, but also the Polish National Cemetery where the Lady in White is spotted (see the story earlier in this chapter), there is an interesting but natural phenomenon that occurs in the cemeteries. Keep in mind these locations are east of the town and the prevailing winds usually blow from west or northwest to the east. It is possible and quite likely that visitors within these cemeteries may hear anomalous voices in these areas that could be quite troubling unless they realize that the sound is traveling on the breezes and winds coming from town or even up the mountain from Lansford.

I verified this explanation on the weekend of the St. Gabriel's Festival in Summit Hill. This festival on the third weekend in July is a major community event. I happened to be in the Polish Cemetery on Ludlow Street that evening and as I was inspecting the area and getting a feeling for the property, I was aware of voices and then music that sounded like it was originating from the building on the property. The voices were almost clear enough to understand (but not totally). It was unnerving until the music started. Once I heard the band play, the sounds made sense. They were not paranormal. They were carried on the breeze from the west end of town to the cemeteries. I have seen this repeated on other evenings in other cemeteries, but the Polish cemetery is the most clear of all of them. I think this is because unlike the other cemeteries, the

Polish one almost sits in a hollow that acts like a collector for sounds and almost amplifies them slightly.

While this explanation works for some of the experiences, I do not think it is adequate enough for the late night bugler in the GAR Cemetery. It would be unusual for someone in town to be blowing Taps at 11pm or midnight and have it waft on the breeze past the GAR to the street. The origin of sound can be deceptive but the officers who are trained to observe details have definitely said the music comes from a point within the cemetery and not from the direction of the town. In the spirit of fairness, I just want to point out that I have yet to hear the phantom bugler myself, but perhaps one evening he may play his song for my benefit.

Brief History of the GAR

When the Civil War ended and the soldiers returned home, they formed a fraternal organization called the Grand Army of Republic. Our local post was E.T. Conner Post 177 named after Lieutenant Colonel Eli T. Conner who died valiantly at Malvern Hill on the evening of June 15, 1862.

Soon after the post formed in 1869, the group purchased four acres from a farm on the east end of Summit Hill and founded the GAR Cemetery in early 1870. One of the first persons buried in it was the first resident of Mauch Chunk Township (which Summit was part of at that time). His name was Josiah White Erskine Hazard George F.A. Hauto Brink.

In total there are 76 known Civil War veterans buried in the GAR Cemetery along with veterans from all wars since then. My grandmother's cousin William Remaley who was lost at sea in World War II is also remembered here with a marker.

When the GAR Post members died, the cemetery was taken over by citizens in the borough and is currently being run by a board of volunteers.

The Opened Grave

Imagine if you will a bright sunny day. The gentle breeze wafting through the trees cools you as the sun tries to warm you while it provides the nurturing for that rich green grass beneath your feet. You are walking a young one, a nephew or a grandson, imparting your wisdom of years of experience as you travel the byways of town. Not even thinking, you decide to take a mid-morning walk through the cemetery.

This description might describe the day James Cunningham took his young grandson for a walk around Summit Hill. As they walked, he decided to take the lad toward the cemeteries perhaps to look at the unusual stones or to use them as a shortcut to head for the woods beyond their location. However, he ended up there, he was not prepared for what was to come. As he walked his young charge through the plots, he noticed some gravediggers opening an area of ground that was close to a familiar plot. In fact, he became agitated as he neared the men when he realized that it should be familiar; familiar because it was his. He sternly demanded to know what authority they had to be there. The men told them they were directed to open this grave. Mr. Cunningham told them there must be some mistake as the grave they were opening belonged to himself. The men were mortified when they realized their error and asked Mr. Cunningham's forgiveness as they located the proper plot on which they were supposed to work

Mr. Cunningham concluded his walk and went home, but he could not shake the horrifying sight from his mind. Seeing your grave opened would be unsettling to anyone, but in his day superstitions and omens could collapse the spirit of the best of men and women. It is believed that perhaps this is what happened to Mr. Cunningham. That night he retired to his bed to get a much-needed rest. Unfortunately that rest became a permanent one because at some point during the night, he passed away. His death was attributed to the agitation and stress from seeing his grave opened.

There is a belief that everything happens for a reason and that Fate can be a cruel mistress. Perhaps this was its way of preparing Mr. Cunningham for what was to shortly happen, or maybe it was just an unfortunate coincidence. That's something each of us will have to decide for ourselves.

Postscript

This story was related to the Summit Hill Historical Society in the late 1990s or early 2000s by Robert Gormley, a lifelong Summit Hill historian who studied the life of James' famous son sculptor Charles Cunningham. Charles was a world renowned anthracite coal sculptor who master the secret of creating sculptures with a sharp, smooth mirror-like surface. The method he used for his famed sculptures was a trade secret he took to his grave, however some have developed theories as to his techniques.

One interested sculptor introduced himself to me at the Summit Hill Historical Society's museum while I was volunteering one summer afternoon. While he was looking at the collection we have on display, he asked me if anyone knew exactly how Cunningham created the marvelous pieces. I had to admit the information we had was sketchy and that no one knew. He said that he believed that what Cunningham did was to use steel wool and emery cloth to polish it and worked his way from larger grades to very fine grades until the surface piece was smoothly polished. Whatever his process was, it made the pieces unique from contemporary sculptors because it did not leave a residue. Most coal carvers end with sculptures that produce coal dust as a residue, but Cunningham managed to use his secret techniques to eliminate this side effect.

Charles Cunningham Photo Gallery-1

Football Award

Baseball Award

Inkwell

The Preserved Boy

The following story was related to me by a lifelong resident of Summit Hill who I met at the Summit Hill Historical Society's meeting when we formed the organization. As I was researching material for the ghost tour we were going to use for a fundraiser, she shared with me this story which she remembered as a youngster being discussed in town.

"Early in the twentieth century, a young man passed away suddenly from an illness and was interred in one of the cemeteries in Summit Hill on a plot purchased quickly so that he could be interred. Several years later, the family decided that a larger family plot was needed, so they arranged to purchase one in another area of that same cemetery. It was arranged that the remains of the boy would be unearthed and moved to the new location so that he could spend eternity with his family when their time came to depart this earthly realm. Two or three gravediggers were hired when the time came for the task."

"First, the men dug the new grave, opening the fresh earth to receive its precious cargo. This was done without too much difficulty on the bright spring morning after the frost melted away in the warmth of the day. Next, they carefully began to remove the dirt covering the casket containing the body of the young man. The work was tricky as they didn't want to hastily dig and damage the protective box, but they also wanted to get the job completed as it was a little unnerving to unearth the tomb. Soon they reached the sarcophagus and as they finished they tied ropes around it and prepared to haul it back to the surface to be taken to the new location. With the ropes securely around the precious cargo, the men slowly but firmly pulled the ropes. To their surprise, the coffin refused to move. They tried again but still it remained firmly in the location it was placed so many years previously."

"Not wanting to be totally defeated, one of the men crawled back into the grave to locate the source of the obstruction. Something holding the coffin against the earth should be noticeable and rectified. A root, perhaps or maybe even a stone against the side they missed. The gravedigger could find nothing amiss. Climbing back to the surface with the help of his companions, the men tried again in vain to remove the casket from the hole. Still their cargo rested in the hole as if the ground refused to yield its treasure. One of the men decided to go find the father of the deceased lad to get his opinion or direction on what to do. The other men waited discussing nervously the apparent force preventing the completion of the task at hand."

"Soon the grave digger returned with the father. He was visibly distraught when he arrived at the gravesite, but he joined the men in another attempt to pull the coffin out of the grave. Still again, it refused to budge even with the four husky men pulling on it. The men stopped after this fruitless attempt and the father made the decision to see what was preventing the box from moving. He climbed down into the grave and examined the exterior of the coffin. Nothing was visible in the hole that could explain the apparent stubbornness. It was at this point the father decided that whatever it was holding the coffin in the hole must be inside the pine box."

He yelled up to the men to get a pry bar. Anxiously he waited and soon the man returned handing the bar down to the father. The nervous father pried tentatively at the coffin and eventually the rusted old lock gave way to the pressure. With a creak, the coffin lid opened in the ground and the father was momentarily shocked at what he saw inside. There in the coffin was his son perfectly preserved as if he had been just buried, but the corpse appeared to be solid stone! The men were horrified for a few minutes at the unexpected sight, but as reason slowly overtook all of them, they tried to determine how the boy could have turned to stone.

The answer was forthcoming in the examination of the opened casket. The men discovered that the box developed a rupture that allowed an underground spring to flow freely through the boy's resting place bathing his body in the mineral rich waters. This prolonged exposure over time calcified or petrified the body. It is said that the body was so perfectly preserved it could have stood in a museum as a statue.

After examining the coffin and fixing what they could, the men moved the body and then the coffin to the newly opened grave on the family plot and reinterred the boy. It is said that the area of the cemetery where this had occurred was never used again to inter a body.

Postscript

I have tried to find another source for this story over the years since it was first told to me by a reliable person in the Historical Society. It is the only tale in this volume, which is not a ghost story per se, but is more one of a shocking occurrence in the cemetery. The woman who shared it attests to it being a true story, but due to her age at the time it took place she does not really remember which cemetery in which this occurred. She believes it might have been St. Joseph's Cemetery but it is not known for sure. I do remember a natural spring that would bubble up along Ludlow Street near St. Michael's Cemetery and St. John the Baptist Byzantine Catholic Cemetery.

While I have not yet found a news source for the Summit Hill Petrified Boy, there is a story in the Milwaukee Journal from February 24, 1903 that documents a petrified coffin. The remains were to be removed to a different cemetery from their original resting place seventeen years earlier in a grave in Wells, Minnesota. It was moved around the turn of the twentieth century to Milwaukee, Wisconsin, but when the grave was opened the coffin was found to be turned to stone. The grave diggers did not realize this and thought it was a metal coffin, but when it arrived in Milwaukee, the sexton saw it was really petrified. It took ten men to return it to the ground according to the news story and it was estimated to weigh over 1500 pounds. The cemetery in Wells was in a low lying area, and it is believed the coffins there were regularly immersed in mineral water creating the bizarre conditions[3].

A search of the Internet reveals that this is only a sample of similar news stories from early 1900's newspapers of petrified bodies. In all of them the explanation is similar to the one given by my storyteller friend. The bodies were laid to rest in the path of a natural spring which over the years slowly ran a mineral bath over the coffins and their contents until they turned the corpses and the coffins into a stone much in the way one would grow crystals as an experiment. While not a ghost story, it definitely is a shocking tale that is part of the fabric of Summit Hill's oral history.

The Animated Soldier

Doughboy Soldier in St. John's Byzantine Catholic Cemetery

World War One was a bloody war fought in the trenches dug across the flat countryside of Europe. Four million plus of our young men traveled across the vast ocean to fight in this war against Germany, Austria and Hungary. Many sacrificed their young lives to win that "War to End All Wars". This left holes in many of the families back home in the United States and probably caused much sorrow and grief. There is a monument to one of our local sons who did not make it home from the war. It stands in St. John the Baptist Byzantine Catholic Cemetery between East White Street and East Ludlow Street and is so distinctive that it cannot be missed. It is a close to life-size replica of a doughboy, and local legend claims that it is a likeness of the hero who gave his life on Europe's bloody battlefields. The story is that the parents were so grief stricken that they commissioned the monument as a lasting tribute to their son.

As one stands outside the cemetery on the Ludlow Street side, the monument is quite distinctive among the normal markers. There are few statues in the cemeteries and this one is unique in that it does not look like an angel or have been influenced by Greek type sculptures with the long flowing robes and such. In fact, this statue is quite true-to-life and looks exactly like a doughboy

39

dressed in a traditional WWI Army uniform. If the actual statue is life-size, then its human model was about five-foot-tall, but I think it might be a scaled down replica of a normal human. Legend has it that the grieving parents commissioned the statue to be a duplicate of their son. The soldier in the monument resembles a seventeen or eighteen-year old which would match the legend. Viewed close up, the statue is an impressive, loving tribute to a long-lost son, however when we step away things become a bit different.

There are two stories that are popular in town in relation to "the doughboy". The first tale is that he smokes. It is said if you take a cigarette to the cemetery and place it between his lips and walk away the statue will soon appear to smoke a cigarette. In fact, a friend once related to me this tale.

"I was at the cemetery with a group of friends. We stood outside the gates debating who was brave enough to test the smoking story. One friend finally consented to do it. We handed him a lit cigarette. He went into the cemetery, walked up to the statue and placed the cigarette between the soldier's lips. As he turned to leave the cemetery, he heard a male voice say, "Thank You!" A quick inspection revealed no human being standing that close as all of his friends were still outside the gate. We did not go back to that cemetery again."

The second story regards an interesting phenomenon. As the sun sets, the statue seems to become animated in a way. If you travel to the cemeteries just before dusk and station yourself on Ludlow St. to observe the statue, you may find that the statue appears to move slightly--the arms shift position or the eyes move. One would say it was the natural movement of the lengthening shadows on the monument, but others have said the statue seems to move prior to any significant change in the shadows. Sometimes his uniform appears to wrinkle. Does the shadow have a life of its own, or is it all just a grand optical illusion? Go visit it for yourself and see what you think the next time you are in Summit Hil

Postscript

The idea the statue marking John Shubeck's grave is in the likeness of the young man himself is a story that circulated through Summit Hill over the years. I have not been able to prove or disprove this fact, but I have been told by several residents the statue resembles photographs of the young soldier. The legend is that his parents were so distraught at losing their son in the Great War that they commissioned the statue so that they could always see him even though he was no longer with them.

The second legend is the soldier will smoke a cigarette if it is placed in his lips. I am uncertain how this could be possible since the sculpture's mouth cannot hold a cigarette. The possibility exists that those who related witnessing this story may have seen the cigarette smoke while someone was holding it to the lips of the soldier, but they would have had to hold it there. While that could be a possibility, I find it unlikely that if a statue started to puff on a cigarette, someone would be able to keep their composure long enough to really make sure before they fled. Because of the physical inability to place a cigarette in the statue's lips, it becomes almost impossible to verify this legend.

I have tried to find another source for this story, and I have tried to watch the statue around dusk over several evenings. He really does appear to move. Whether this is supernatural or not, I really do not know right now. A natural explanation could be that as the sun sets, the shadows cast on objects also change in size. It is possible that the shifting of shadows may account for his movements, except sometimes people who have encountered this unusual situation do not wait for the amount of time it would take shadows to move. In fact, they can see the statue alter its position and return to the original stance in seconds. Does the statue have a life of its own? We will never know for sure, but maybe when you see it yourself, you can determine the secret of how it moves on its own.

The Unknown Soldier of Summit Hill

Most towns have their unsung heroes and Summit Hill is no different. At one time during the mining days of Summit Hill a stagecoach road ran through the town entering up the southern side of the mountain running along the ridge and then crossing near the quarry to a home down on West Holland Street. This home which still has its broad wrap-around porch at that time was a stagecoach stop, so it is logical that people coming and going from town would meet here to catch a ride. It would not be unusual to find strangers in this area but one man made his presence known in a unique way.

Late one night in early April 1861 there was a fierce storm. The rain poured and the wind howled as the storm pounded the town. Early the next morning, Mrs. Smith went to the well near the stagecoach stop to get some water for the daily chores. She removed the cover and began to draw water when she ran into a problem. The bucket was stuck. No matter how hard she pulled, the bucket would not free itself. Finally, she sought out help from a few men who lived nearby[4].

Together the group was able to get the bucket to move but it was like pulling a stone up from the bottom of the well. As it came into view, they all learned why the bucket had such an unusual weight to it. A little old man dressed in an Army uniform was draped over the bucket. He was quite waterlogged and deceased. The cause of death was not known, but it was said that he probably died from falling and hitting his head on the well wall or the ground.

They examined the man's body and in one of the coat pockets they found his identification papers from the US Army. Unfortunately due to his evening misadventure the well-water soaked papers were mostly illegible. Authorities were able to tell he served during the Mexican War and was discharged in 1846, but that was the only information they could glean from the waterlogged documents. The town was soon buzzing with this gruesome discovery, yet no one could figure out who he was.

Finally, the Presbyterian Church in town offered to bury him in their cemetery. They buried him two days later with full military honors and the funeral attracted several local dignitaries including a local attorney, the local boy scouts and one Father Kelly. He has not been disturbed from his resting place and to this day, it never was determined who the man was or why he was in the well that night. One question was never answered though—why was the well covered the next morning? It's an answer that will never be given I suppose, but we can wonder.

Postscript

There are a pair of stories I have found in two different newspapers that discuss the Unknown Soldier of Summit Hill. One from 1927 in the Reading Eagle and the other was a Morning Call story in the 1960s that discuss this veteran interred in the old Presbyterian cemetery which is now a park located at Market Street between Hazard and Fell streets. The former story gives more perspective on the man and why he may have been in Summit Hill, but the latter story provides critical information that will help the soldier finally rest in peace with the recognition and honor he deserves.

Summit Hill Presbyterian Cemetery, Early 1900's

The first account of this man was in a story in the Reading Eagle which appeared on June 12, 1927.[5] In this article, the reporter writes the man was attired in a Civil War uniform for the Northern Army. He was wounded but unable to give a coherent account of who he was or what happened to him. The reporter describes the man as having worked odd jobs through the community, but was never willing to accept charity for his work. He apparently slept in the coach stables and was missing for a week before they searched for him. It was as a result of this search he was found in the well. He was buried in the cemetery with full honors and service provided the Eli T. Conner Post of the GAR and his grave was tended until the turn of the century after which the ongoing care ended. In the article, the American Legion agreed to take over the care for this gentleman, but the story made it clear that no one knew who this man was.

A few years after the stories in this book were originally written, the Summit Hill Historical Society undertook a project to replace the soldier's stone in the park. In the intervening years between when the cemetery closed and was converted to a park and the Society formed, the grave marker had been lost. During their research into the soldier, one member uncovered an article written in 1937 in the Allentown Morning Call newspaper regarding an investigative report that was done with regard to the "man in the well" or Summit Hill's "Unknown Soldier". It turns out the investigative reporter was able to identify this mystery man in the well. The reporter revealed the man's name to be Frederick Leiber. The Society was finally able to give the man a fitting marker and a re-dedication service worthy of a veteran. The stone joins one of three erected in the park on Market Street.

The Phantom Owner

At the end of East White Street in the borough of Summit Hill is an unassuming office surrounded by granite and marble monuments named Walter's Monument Company. The business is owned by Craig Walters, a well respected businessman in the community who has managed the business for over 25 years. He learned the monument business from the ground up while working for the previous owners, Bronne and Mary Bruzgo from whom he bought the business in the early 1990s before her death.

Like other businesses, the monument business is a seasonal one. Its busiest time is the month or two before Memorial Day which is one holiday set aside to remember those who died for our country. It has also expanded since its inception as a national holiday to a time where many remember their loved ones. One of the primary ways most people do that is through headstones and grave markers. Walters uses granite and marble shipped in from New England daily. From March to May, it is not unusual for Walters and his employees to be working eighteen hours daily to be ready for installations prior to Memorial Day. This schedule is an integral part of the business which he learned from Mary when he started working there at the age of 19.

It was one such evening that found Walters working late in the workshop on one of these many monuments. Due to the naturally dusty work caused from cutting and preparing stone, some of the dirtier equipment is partitioned off into smaller areas off of the main workshop. In one of the back corners is a room he built to do stenciling and engraving near where the wire saw is used. This room was partitioned out of a large workshop area by Craig just to contain the work.

Craig was in this area getting ready to finish for the night when he felt a cold breeze on his face. It caught him by surprise and he turned toward the door of this room and all of a sudden the hairs on the back of his arms stood up. He could feel the energy all around the front of him. There in the dim light about ten feet from the door was a figure sitting in a chair.

"The shape was a man but it was a shadow. I couldn't see any features," Craig said when he told the story. He said the man was sitting down. He appeared to have a fedora on his head and was motionless. Startled at seeing this apparition Craig said the figure was there and then slowly faded from sight along with the spectral chair. He did not panic as he cautiously moved past the area where the figure was sitting, but he did carefully and swiftly wind down the nightly operations and left.

"A few days later I mentioned this odd encounter to my employees," Walters remembered. At the time no one said anything. An old colleague of his who retired from the shop stopped by later for a visit. Patty was a veteran of the Bruzgo ownership and spent years working in the workshop. Craig related the story to the older man describing the shadow, the fedora and the location in the shop.

Patty listened and when Craig finished, he said in his gruff style. "You never saw the old man, did you?"

Craig said, "No. I started working when Mrs. Bruzgo was the owner."

"Well, let me tell you something," he replied. "That old man in that fedora you described sitting in the chair? That's the old man you saw. He used to sit there watching us when he was in the shop right in the spot you described—wearing that hat."

Craig was incredulous. "That was the old man?" Patty said, "Yep." Craig invited him back to see a monument on which we was working, but the old employee refused to go back into the shop. He said that Patty never set foot in the shop after that.

Several nights later, Craig was at home relaxing when the phone rang. He answered it hearing a breathless voice of one of his employees on the other end.

"What's wrong?", Craig asked.

The man caught his breath and said, "Craig! I was just in the shop working on that order. I started feeling anxious and the air felt heavy. I got the unnerving feeling that I was being watched. That's when I looked up."

"That old man was sitting there staring back at me," the employee said fervently, "he was wearing the hat and everything just like you said! The friggin' hair was standing up on the back of my arms and I couldn't look away from him."

Craig asked if he was okay. The employee replied, "Yes. It's over now but let me tell you one thing. I'm not working in that fuckin' shop ever again at night. Don't even ask me to!"

The employee stayed true to his word and never stayed late into the evening again. According to Craig almost every employee has seen Mr. Bruzgo in the workshop over the years. His son told me that when he is there in the evenings, he sometimes gets the feeling that people are in the offices moving around and has seen shadows of people occasionally in the business.

Mr. Bruzgo was passionate about his business in life and even though he is dead for almost 40 years, his spirit apparently still worries about his life's work. So much so, that he continues to offer his guidance apparently even if only from beyond the grave.

Postscript

Bronne Bruzgo was a driven man who built his company from the ground up when he first opened in 1920. While there is some uncertainty as to whether he purchased the business from banker Charles Benson Adams or opened it on his own, what is undisputed is that Mr. Bruzgo quickly built it into a thriving successful business that reached far beyond the borough of Summit Hill.

In a short time, the company was the largest employer in Summit Hill and reportedly the largest monument company on the East Coast. He was embroiled in several scandals over the years

Bronne Bruzgo poses near monument for a news story in Morning Call (Kreamer, 1954)

including being accused of underselling monuments while competing with smaller companies. By the mid 1950s, his two sons Robert and Bronne were officers in the business. They came under fire for tax evasion with Robert eventually going to prison. This didn't hinder the business as it continued to grow and thrive even after Mr. Bruzgo's death in 1982.

Mrs. Bruzgo ran the business, but it started to decline due to her love of drink over love of business. The business remained open continuously even as it started to slump until lifelong employee, Craig Walters purchased the business from her in the early 1990's.

Since then Craig has brought the business back to be a thriving regional business with two offices, the main office in Summit Hill and one in Hazleton along with salespeople throughout Pennsylvania. He has modernized the business and now uses CAD technologies to create artistic three-dimensional works of art. Craig's son is also part of the family business, one that shows no signs of stopping. Both men believe Bronne oversees the business not to cause any harm, but as a guiding spirit that protects and watches over his monument empire.

Encounter In An Alley

It was just after midnight in mid-July 2020 on a clear night. Rob Heckman, a local social media weatherman, was on his way home from an evening spent with family in Lehighton. He left there around midnight and stopped at a local convenience store to pick up some milk for the next day. He was in pretty good spirits as he drove in his sportscar with the top down so that he could enjoy the night air and the clear skies. The third quarter moon was just breaking the horizon this night, so the stars were shining brightly

He lived on East Hazard Street and his regular car was parked in front of his house, so he usually parked his sports car in the alley behind it. Rob turned up East White Street and headed toward the cemeteries at the eastern edge of the town. It was just before 1AM as he turned left into the alley passing Walter's Monument Company's shop.

Walter's Monument Company[6] occupies both sides of the alley at the end of East Ridge Street. The company was originally the Summit Hill Marble and Granite Company. It was founded in 1920 by Bronne and Mary Bruzgo and run by the family until it was sold to Craig Walters in the mid-1990s. At one time this company was the largest supplier of cemetery monuments on the East Coast. Mr. Bruzgo ran the company with his two sons, but Mrs. Bruzgo was a fixture in the business and ran it after his death.

The main office faces White Street with the workshops located immediately behind it in two buildings which open into the alley. A roof covers the alley for the width of the buildings creating a covered archway over the end of the cemetery.

It was under this arch that Rob was startled to see an old woman walking slowly toward the cemetery. Her countenance was illuminated by the streetlight as she walked slowly toward the cemetery.

Rob said, "I saw an older woman dressed completely in white in a nightgown like dress. She was in her late sixties or early seventies and was bare footed. She was gray without any color that I noticed."

He said the hair on his arms and neck stood up from the surprise encounter. She did not acknowledge him as she made her slow steady journey. He said his car was noisy, but she didn't even seem momentarily startled by the noise as he turned into the alley. She just kept her gaze fixed toward her destination of the cemetery.

Rob passed her and parked midway down the alley, but his gaze remained transfixed on his rearview mirror. The woman continued walking steadily toward the cemetery. He said she reached the street and did not turn. "She just headed straight toward the cemetery and then she just disappeared." He believed she might have entered a gate but had no idea where she went.

He ran quickly through the house stopping to drop his milk off in the fridge but then headed out the door to his car parked near the cemetery. He was concerned about this barefooted woman as he drove around the corner searching the cemetery and nearby streets for any sign of her, but she was gone.

What was even more mysterious was that when he stopped to check the gate, he realized there was none. The cemetery was fenced in with its only gates on White and Hazard Streets. While the fence was leaning in there was no simple opening to enter. In addition, tombstone blanks were piled about three to four feet high in front of the fence at the point where she vanished. There was no way she could have walked straight into the cemetery as he observed.

Rob told me in closing that it gave him the "heebie-jeebies" and it was only at that point he realized the woman he encountered may have been a ghost. Who she is though remains a mystery; at least for now?

Postscript

This story came to me at an opportune moment to add it to the conclusion of this first chapter. I interviewed Rob almost twelve hours after the incident and he was shaken by the experience. He didn't realize what he saw until after he noticed there was no gate at that part of the fence and that she could not have just entered the cemetery walking straight without negotiating tall stacks of tombstone blanks, a street sign and a bent in fence that would have required someone to navigate through the obstacles. When she just vanished, it shocked him.

I checked with the police to see if there was anyone matching her description living in that end of town. My first thought was that this was an older resident who may have dementia and left her house after midnight in confusion, but Rob said she did not seem confused. She was expressionless and fixated on her destination. The officer told me he only had one call that evening for fireworks on that end of the borough and there were no women of whom they were aware that matched the description in those blocks.

I checked with the monument company and found that their security cameras did pick up a vehicle that matched Rob's making a few passes in the alley shortly after 1AM as well as his original travel down the alley when he saw this stranger. Unfortunately, the camera was angled more to pick up the width of the alley leaving the corner of the arch out of the camera's view. There was a brief anomaly on the footage but nothing that was conclusively out of place.

We researched St. Joseph's Cemetery as well to see if anyone in the first few rows may have ties to the July 11th or 12th date, but unfortunately a search of death certificates for women matching that age resulted in no likely candidates for our mysterious specter. The people buried near the fence where this woman disappeared do not seem to match the description of age that Rob provided.

There is one other explanation which I am attempting to prove as this book is being published. When I spoke to the owner's son who works there in the shop with his father, he told me that there are times when he is there in the evening after the office staff has left for the day, he will see people or shadows moving around in the front of the building between the rooms. It does not bother him anymore and he has never seen anything more than that. He just described a feeling of being watched occasionally.

Could the older woman be the Summit Hill Marble and Granite Company's former owner, Mary Bruzgo[7]? Everyone who knew her expressed intense emotions. She was a "force of nature" to put it mildly. People with whom I have spoken who were contemporaries of hers stated that she could be cantankerous and mean especially when she was drinking which she did frequently.

Those strong emotions may attach her to the property she spent years overseeing. It is possible that she checks on her former business periodically like her husband is reportedly doing. And maybe just by pure chance, her spirit was spotted by a startled young man returning to his home as she returned to her home in the cemetery. A chance encounter in a dark alley in the middle of the night that will forever be a mystery in search of an explanation.

CHAPTER TWO

Ghost Stories About Town

At one time Summit Hill had many landmarks including an armory, five hotels, at least two supermarkets, a movie theater, three schools and many other buildings and residences. Over the years while many communities were able to hang onto their unique buildings, Summit Hill's buildings fell victim to various natural enemies--neglect, fire and the wrecking ball. Even though some of the buildings are nothing but memories, the experiences and anecdotes that people remember are still popular tales in groups. In this chapter we will explore these tales of the strange.

The Hero's Farewell

Radioman First Class William D. Remaley (Photograph: www.OnEternalPatrol.com)

World War Two saw several of Summit Hill's finest young men travel to the battlefields of Europe and the islands in the Pacific to defend democracy against the evil of tyranny. Many of our sons made it home, but unfortunately too many boys died or were missing in action and never recovered. My great-great Aunt Emma Remaley had a son named William Remaley who fought in the South Pacific aboard the original USS Gudgeon, a submarine, which single handedly sunk over 500,000 lbs. of Japanese tonnage during twelve missions.

My great aunt Esther Remaley and my great grandmother Hazel Remaley lived just around the corner from my Aunt Emma during the early part of the century, and my Aunt Esther was a close friend to her cousin Bill. They corresponded often to share information about the events around them. This is the story as related by my Aunt Esther.

"One morning in the spring of 1944, a huckster named Pete, the Banana Man, made his weekly run from Jim Thorpe to Summit Hill to sell fruits and vegetables to the townspeople. Like most farmers of his day, he would set up shop from his truck at different locations on the streets in town for the citizens to come and buy their goods. Usually he would come down Oak Street, a main thoroughfare at that time, and stop near my mother's home. After selling his wares there, he would continue to the corner and turn right onto Fell Street stopping near my Aunt Emma's house to sell fruit to those neighbors. This day Aunt Emma must have been watching for him and as he made his customary Oak Street stop, she quickly made her way up the backyard, out the back gate and down the alley to meet him at my mother's home. She bought her produce and tarried until the rest of the neighbors left along with the huckster before turning to mother and me. She told us she had to tell us something."

"We were wondering what she could possibly tell us as she began. My aunt said that she had turned in the previous night and was sleeping comfortably in bed when she heard a faint cry, "Mother, Mother…" A disembodied voice roused her from her peaceful slumber continually crying, "Mother! Mother!" As she stirred, the voice became more urgent and a figure materialized near the bed calling to her. It was her son, Bill, who was physically in the South Pacific, but for some reason, she could now see him calling her urgently. She answered and he seemed to calm, but she got an uneasy feeling from the apparition. She said he told her that he was going to be okay and not to worry. As she watched the apparition began to fade, she called back to him, "Billy, Billy…", but the figure dissolved into the inky night. She felt strongly at that point that something terrible had happened and Bill was lost. She settled back down into an uneasy sleep and did not stir until morning. She was not sure what to say, but after thinking about it for the day, she felt like she had to tell someone, hence the reason for her visit. After some more small talk, Aunt Emma left the porch and returned home."

"The incident was forgotten in our house as we went about our business, but one day a few weeks later, Aunt Emma stopped around the house. We could tell immediately by the look on her face and the yellow note in her hand that something terrible had happened. We asked her in and offered her a seat which she accepted. In her hand was a telegram from the War Department. She handed it to us as she said, 'It really was him. He must have come to tell me good-bye.' We looked at the telegram together and almost immediately, it hit us like a pile of bricks. The USS Gudgeon was lost at sea. All hands aboard were MIA and presumed dead. Our sorrow for my cousin hit hard, but not as hard as the next thing I noticed. The date the Gudgeon was lost was the same date that Aunt Emma had claimed to have her visit from her son. He really did come to say good-bye."

An interesting footnote to this story inadvertently occurred about forty-seven years later. We were having a community yard sale when a stranger approached us and asked about Aunt Emma. We informed him she had passed away several years ago, and he told us he had visited her in the early sixties. He had worked for the War Department during the World War II and was involved in the monitoring of the Naval fleet and its accomplishments during the war. He offered his condolences once again to her on her loss, but he felt the need to tell

THE USS GUDGEON

The USS Gudgeon was a Tambor class submarine that was first launched on January 25, 1941 prior to the beginning of the War in the Pacific.

It undertook its first war patrol on December 11, 1941 four days after the dawn attack on Pearl Harbor by the Japanese, an attack which pulled the United States into World War II and was the cause of President Franklin D. Roosevelt's "Infamy" speech.

For the next two and a half years, the Gudgeon was one of several submarines that took advantage of the Japanese Navy's inability or unwillingness to provide proper escorts for its shipping. The Gudgeon itself was responsible for damaging and sinking a total of 115,147 tons of Japanese ships over the course of eleven war patrols.

The ship left on its twelfth patrol from the Marianas Islands on April 4, 1944 and was officially considered overdue on June 7, 1944. Later research done by author Mike Ostlund has determined that it is likely the Gudgeon was sunk by a Japanese submarine killer on April 18, 1944 north of the Marianas Islands. No one survived. (Ostlund, 2014)

her what he understood had happened to the submarine upon which Bill died. The stranger then related this story to us as we listened intently.

He said that during the war it was not uncommon for submarines to sneak behind enemy lines for reconnaissance and disruption of supply lines. The USS Gudgeon had several successful tours of duty performing such maneuvers. This night in May, however, they were fired upon by a Japanese destroyer and ended up disabled near the coast of Southeast Asia in the South China Sea. One of our destroyers was close by, but due to the presence of Japanese ships, the destroyer could not rescue the men in the vessel. Rather than allow the submarine to fall into enemy hands, a fate worse than death for the submariners, the Navy scuttled and sunk the submarine by gunfire. All hands aboard were lost. (Submariners were tortured and abused horribly by Japanese. The atrocities committed against them sometimes came close to those who suffered at the hands of the Nazis). This information was shared with her at that point only because it had recently become declassified. He said my aunt was grateful for his honesty and his willingness to find her and tell her the story.

Postscript

NH 65646 USS GUDGEON (SS 211) Official U.S. Navy photograph, courtesy of Naval History and Heritage Command.

About six years ago, I was researching World War II stories online when I came across a book called "Find 'Em, Chase 'Em, Sink 'Em" by author Mike Ostlund whose uncle, Lieutenant Junior Grade William C. Ostlund was one of the 79 men lost on the submarine when it was declared missing and likely sunk on April 18, 1944. I purchased the book and eagerly read the entire work over the course of the week after I received it. Amazingly, my cousin Bill is mentioned only in the final pages of the tale, but the incident is quite interesting considering the family tale handed down from generation to generation.

It appears Bill was troubled on the evening prior to leaving port on what would be the final patrol of the Gudgeon. He was found down by the dock by a former submarine mate Art Barlow who was transferred off of the Gudgeon. According to Ostlund's book, Barlow tried to reassure Bill that everything would be just fine, but Bill would not be consoled. He told him that this was the final patrol and that they would not be returning.

The next page revealed another interesting item. Former skipper Bill Post revealed in an article in The Dolphin in 1982 that around the time the USS Gudgeon was lost, he had "an overwhelming premonition" that the ship and its crew was lost at sea. He does not elaborate in the article what that premonition

David A. Wargo

was, but Ostlund wrote that it was not unusual for sailors and ships to have such extrasensory connections. (Ostlund, 2014)

I got in touch with Mike Ostlund to find out if these men were still alive and related my family story to him. He sadly told me I missed speaking to both men by a year or two as they had passed away. I speculated with Mike that perhaps the skipper knew because not only did he have a feeling, but maybe because he had a vision of his former radioman like the one my Aunt Emma had. Unfortunately, the answer to that question remains an eternal enigma

A Premonition?

My cousin Bill Remaley became the radioman on the Gudgeon on March 8, 1943 when he transferred from the USS Triton to the USS Gudgeon.

He was home prior to this assignment a final time. During his visit, he helped his dad with fix the roof of their house. He was fooling around on the ladder and Emma chided him to be careful. He replied, "It won't matter, I'm not going to be around long anyway." She dismissed the comment at the time, but later recalled it to my great-grandmother.

As the end of his leave drew near,, my great aunt Esther Parkinson told me that he was reluctant to leave. With regard to his final night at home, she said, "We sat up and talked all night and I could tell he was apprehensive about returning to the war."

They spent most of that last night on the back porch visiting and talking and he left the next morning. He would never return to his home again. Her final letter was returned to her in the summer of 1944 after the ship was lost at sea.

A total of 79 men lost their lives that morning on the USS Gudgeon and each one was a true American hero.

58

Other Night Visitors

I remember my Aunt Emma Remaley as a kind, gentle woman. She would visit our house and sit in a rocking chair my mother kept in the kitchen for her. I was about nine years old when she died.

Many years after she passed, I learned that we were living in her home. She and her husband Harvey owned our house for decades before she sold it to my mom and dad. She surprised them one evening by asking them to visit. When they arrived, she asked them to sit down and proposed they buy her house.

She said, "I will be leaving a few doors away with my sisters, but if you owned the house, I can still return to visit my home." My parents discussed it and decided they would accept her offer.

Our house has a rich family history. My great-great grandfather Daniel Remaley and my great uncle Harvey Remaley both were laid out in our living room when they died. Older generations of our family spent much time there in during Aunt Emma's life--not all of them may have necessarily been living.

My Aunt Emma claimed to have several deceased family members visit her at night, but her son Bill only visited once to our knowledge. My Aunt Esther Parkinson said that Emma often spoke of her father, Wallace appearing at night to speak with her. Another frequent night visitor was her husband Harvey. I never got a chance to ask my great-great aunt about these experiences as she died when I was only eight years old, but it is possible based on our experiences that these visits may not be so far-fetched. Our family has had several experiences through the years that might support Emma's claims to my Aunt Esther.

My mother shared a story about a nighttime visit she and my father have not forgotten. They recently moved into the house when my great grandfather Alex Harvilla on my father's side suddenly became deathly ill. My parents visited him regularly and one evening after their visit they came home and went to bed. During the middle of the night they woke to an unusual noise. My mother was roused from sleep by the sound of the back door being opened downstairs. She shook my dad awake and told him what she heard. He jumped out of bed with her behind to see what was happening. They noticed it was about four in the morning.

They silently moved through the home searching each room in turn for the invader but as they reached the kitchen to their surprise, they found the door was stills securely locked. They were surprised and my mother swore to my father she heard the door opening prior to waking him. My parents returned to bed but were unable to sleep well the rest of the night. When they finally woke the next morning, they received a phone call from my grandmother. My dad's grandfather passed away during the night around 4AM. To this day, my parents believe the door opening was him coming to say good-bye one last time.

Twenty-four years passed and this phenomenon repeated itself to my parents with my dad's father but instead of happening at his death, it occurred about twelve hours before he passed. It was mid-June in 1980 and my grandfather had a stroke and was admitted to the hospital. The toll of mining on his lungs and his heart were finally wreaking havoc on him and as he failed, my parents and my grandmother were at the hospital as much as possible. On the evening before he passed away, I remember my parents gathering us in their bedroom to share with us that he was going to die soon. It was the first time we would experience losing a grandparent, so my mother wanted us to be prepared.

Since school was out for the summer, we went to bed around 10:30 that night and my parents, exhausted from the hospital visits, retired soon afterward. Around 3AM, they woke to hear the back door open and close. My father investigated and found the door was locked tight and no one was there just like twenty-four years ago. My parents and grandmother returned to the hospital in the morning and spent a good part of the day with him. They left in the middle of the afternoon to return home, but unfortunately they were only home for a minute or two when the hospital called that he was dying. By the time they got back to the hospital, he already died. Interestingly, one of my grandfather's sisters said during the gathering they too had the experience of hearing a door open and close twelve hours before my grandfather's death. Perhaps he was making his rounds to say one final good-bye.

While I never shared that experience, I had a few of my own as I was growing up there. The first occurred when I was about four or five years old. I was outside playing on our porch. It was late afternoon and my mother was cooking dinner in the kitchen. My father was working that day and was not yet home. As I played on the porch, I heard a male voice say, "David." I looked around and I heard it once again. "David!" Yet there was no one there.

I opened the door and went inside and asked my mother, "Is dad home?"

She said, "No. He's still at work, but he should be home soon. Why do you ask?"

I told her that I thought I heard him calling my name, but she said that it must have been my imagination and at that point the conversation ended. I never brought it up to her again, but the experience occurred one more time. I was thirteen and this time it was late evening in the summer. My mother just tucked us into bed, and I was beginning to sleep when the voice returned, I heard an unmistakable "David!" My mind snapped to attention and I looked for the source, but there was no one there. Once again, my father was at work and there was no one there. When I realized it was the same person again, I was not scared. I felt safe and secure, so I just closed my eyes and went back to sleep.

Several times during my childhood, I heard a man's voice call my name from the porch and my bedroom. The voice was not recognizable, but it was a strong male voice. In the evenings when I heard it, I would already be in bed. I do know that my dad was never home when this happened and there were no other adult men in the house when I would hear it speak my name. I do know that it was not a figment of my imagination, but it was an enigma that has even puzzled me even until now. There was one other incident that occurred, but for several years I thought it was my imagination playing tricks on me, yet something happened recently to make me rethink the whole thing.

When I was a child, I would get deathly ill sometimes with a high fever. In fourth grade, it was determined that my tonsils were severely infected and would need to be removed. After that was completed, my health greatly improved, but from time to time I was still susceptible to illness and fevers. In fifth grade during the early spring, I once again developed a high fever that was at least 103. After a few days of this elevated temperature, my parents took me to the doctor for a shot of penicillin. Once they brought me home, they tucked me into bed and warned me not to take the blankets off of me as my fever should soon start to break, and they wanted me to sweat it out of my system. My mother kissed me on the forehead and said good night to me, then she turned on the lamp on my nightstand and turned off the big overhead light. The light was just to my left on the nightstand near my bed, and it was strong enough to illuminate the room so that no shadows were present. To the immediate left of the nightstand was the bedroom door, and to the right of my bed was a door to the closet that was shared with my brother. It was about ten PM when she left me to fight my fever with this inoculation. I eventually drifted into a light, troubled sleep.

Sometime during the night, I can remember regaining consciousness long enough to look around the room. I was semi-conscious as I looked around the room, first to the right then to the left. As I looked to the left, I noticed a shadow which initially appeared to be on the door, but as I looked at it longer, it looked more like it was in front of the door. The shadow was in the shape of a man who was between five foot eight and six foot tall, but it was essentially featureless. It was almost like looking at a shadow left behind by a person, yet there was no person in my room to account for this shape. I can remember looking at it and then looking back to the other side of the room before closing my eyes and going back to sleep.

For years, I didn't really think any further about it, but when my brother started experiencing "visitors" at his parsonage of his church, I asked him about our homestead. We met for lunch one day, and I said to him, "Did you have anything strange happen to you in the house while we were growing up?" He told me that he locked the doors one evening and went to take a shower. As he washed, he could swear he heard the door open, so he left the shower and with a towel wrapped around him, he searched the house. No one was there, but the locked back door was standing wide open. He also had multiple experiences with the light in the kitchen turning itself off without human hands. I said to him that I was aware of those things and then rephrased my question to be: "Did you ever see anything strange in the house?"

At that point, my brother became elusive and asked me, "Why? What did you see?"

I answered, "If I tell you, will you tell me?" He answered affirmatively, so I related the story about my fever and the figure that made a brief appearance in the doorway. As I finished, he looked like he was in shock, so I asked him what was wrong. He said, "David, that was the same figure I saw throughout high school and college in my dreams. I would dream that I was in my cradle and I would look up and see the shadow of a man standing over me. For years, I didn't understand it, but now it makes more sense. He sounds exactly like your description."

This probably would not be such a big deal in most cases, however this was the first time I had ever told another living person about the experience and for my brother to have the same experiences twelve years previously is a bit strange. We have not been able to determine exactly who the figure is, but apparently both of us on separate occasions have witnessed this apparition in the back bedroom of the house. The reason is when my brother was a baby his nursery was the back room that later became my bedroom; at that point I was in the room that became his bedroom. His cradle sat on the wall that my bed was on years later when I had my experience. Perhaps one of my aunt's late-night visitors was checking up on us periodically, or maybe he was looking for my aunt and did not realize she no longer lived at our house.

The figure did return last winter though. My father sleeps in the front bedroom. He told me that something woke him around two in the morning. He sat up and waited a moment but there were no sounds. He decided to get up to get a drink of water from the bathroom. My father sleeps on the side of the bed away from the door so he stood up and walked around the ends of the bed until he was in line with the doorway. As he reached the door he looked up and noticed a figure bathed in white light leave the rear bedroom and cross the end of the hall into the stairwell. My father hurried down the hall but whatever was there vanished. He got his drink of water and went back to bed. It may be a coincidence, but the date of this encounter corresponds with my cousin Bill's birthday on January 2nd. Perhaps he came home for a visit one more time. It just so happened this time my father was lucky enough to see him return home for a visit.

The Cursed Payroll

Being a center of coal mining, Summit Hill was like the old west of the east. Coal miners were a rough lot and there were fights and violence besides the prosperity in this community. Several murders have been recorded in the 1800s and early 1900s in this town, some of which were attributed to misadventure and some were quite deliberate. Such was the case of the deliberate assassination of one Joseph Zehner and Samuel Watkins. In those days, the men were often paid in gold coins. The weekly payroll was distributed to the mines from the main office in Summit Hill: this one was bound for Nesquehoning. One account of the incident written in the Reading Eagle the day after the double murders stated that Watkins was not the original driver. His brother Benjamin was Zehner's regular driver, but Samuel was on holiday and wanted to see the strip-mining operations so he eagerly volunteered to substitute that fateful morning.[8]

**Kitchen Road (Hell's Kitchen Road) looking east near St. Joseph's Cemetery
(Photo by author)**

Early on Thursday morning September 7, 1911, Zehner and Watkins loaded the payroll of between $4000-4200 into the wagon and secured it[9], then set forth from Summit Hill along the Kitchen Road[10] that began at the east end of Hazard Street and ran behind the cemeteries along the mountain ridge to Nesquehoning. They were never seen alive again.

A portion of the Kitchen Road still exists along the left-hand side of the GAR and St. Joseph's Cemeteries, but the rest of the road is long since reclaimed by the forest. This route was considered extremely dangerous for more than one reason. First the natural dangers along that road were the black circular vent holes for the mines in Nesquehoning. These vents led to the surface near the road after you passed where the tower lines are now. They are even more dangerous today as they are open and at least 1200 feet deep. A stone tossed from the top never is heard to hit the bottom. The second hazard was a human one in the form of bandits and thieves who would attack travelers on the road especially in the evenings or at night. The road was given a suitable nickname--"Hell's Kitchen Road".

Sometime shortly after noon, a party on an automobile excursion on the Kitchen road discovered the wagon in a clearing near the Black Rocks just on the other side of Little Italy outside of Nesquehoning.[11] The horse was quietly eating grass near the wagon. The men had been killed by gunshots. Zehner had been shot through the neck while Watkins was shot in the left temple. The payroll chest was still in the wagon supposedly covered with the men's blood. There was no sign of the assassins.

Since the murders took place near Little Italy, the police immediately issued a general notice that any suspicious men should be apprehended for questioning. Later that day in Parryville, two Italian immigrants were caught trying to board a New York bound train. They were kept for questioning and after their interrogations they were released. One might say this was a case of prejudicial profiling and we would agree if not for the fact that soon after their both men were killed in mining accidents[12].

Jumping ahead several years, Jay Frantz wrote a column in the Valley Gazette, a local newspaper that published news and coal region nostalgia. Frantz wrote that when he was a child, he and his friends witnessed the escaping murderers while they were playing. He claimed they heard the shots echo in the Valley and soon after saw two men fleeing along the road to Summit Hill. The boys ran away and hid for days until the men were apprehended for fear that they may have been seen by the assassins.

There is an old Italian custom that states that money tainted with spilled blood is cursed and would bring misfortune to those who come in contact with it. Perhaps it is this curse that meted out the ultimate reward to the two men. Of course, maybe something else scared these murderers before they could complete their theft. Unfortunately what really happened that day rests in the souls of two long dead assassins who never profited from their crime.

Postscript

An account related to me said the horses had appeared to drag the cart in a circle in the clearing causing a deep rut in the soft dirt. It seemed that the horse somehow was forced to pull the wagon in a circle for a few hours before it finally broke free. It was later found near Summit Hill.

When we compiled the first ghost tour, one of the local historical society members recounted to me that the men were buried in two cemeteries, the Grand Army Cemetery and the old Presbyterian Cemetery simultaneously. She said the bells on the churches tolled as the caskets were lowered into the ground.

In researching the postscript for this story, I found that the story has several different versions, but they all provide some basic shared details. The men were murdered delivering the payroll. Two men were sought for the crimes but ultimately never stood trial. Both men died a short time later. The proverbial devil is in the details. Some accounts say the money was stolen while others say some or all of it was intact. Some accounts freed the two suspects while others state they were released due to insufficient evidence. Even their fates are not totally certain.

The two men who stood accused of the crime based on circumstantial evidence according to a retrospective article from the Mauch Chunk Times News in 1943[13] were Paul Musatchia and Philip Faraja. Mustachia was later found dead in a stripping pit in 1913 of a broken neck after a landslide.

Faraja's fate is totally unknown. He disappeared from any official record; however local tales claim he may have been killed in New York within two years as well. Even the historical record is surrounded with unanswered questions and makes this tale a true mystery.

The Mourning Land

Behind the Ginter stadium is a hill made from landfill that was moved into the quarry during the 1980s. At one time the area on the southwest part of the town was a deep quarry scarring the land from the removal of coal during the 1800s. In the mid-1800s, flooding and a mine fire almost brought the quarry operation to a complete standstill. The quarry operation never fully recovered after this. By the early part of the century, the area behind the stadium looked like it was subjected to a massive bomb blast. It was scarred by the environmental damage with no trees and vegetation, but its desolation held darker secrets.

The stadium was nestled at the base of the southern mountaintop bordered on the south by the ridge, the east and north by the town and the west by a deep pit. Imagine climbing to the top of the open-air metal bleachers on the west edge of the complex, the brown painted steel protecting you from the one-hundred-foot drop. Looking west you see a deep hole for

Ginder, Ginter or Ginther?

Summit Hill was founded in the area near where Philip Ginder discovered anthracite coal rock on the ground in 1791. The town formed first as a patch town in the early 1800's and became a borough in 1889. Ginder eventually left the area, but his name stayed near the place he discovered coal.

When the town built a new high school in 1927, they named it Philip Ginter High School. After the school was named, there was a controversy over the spelling that actually ended up in court. The court declared that the name is really "Ginder" and that Ginter was an Americanized version that should not be used in reference to the man.

Today the town's monument still shows the correct spelling as do our history books. The stadium near the place where the school originally stood until it burned in 1971 still bears the name Ginter Stadium and is the town's recreational complex.

What was never correct was a typo on a poster in the early 2000s that spelled the name "Ginther". To be clear, that name was and is not an acceptable variation of the name. Ginder is the man and Ginter is the stadium.

miles stretching beneath the ridge as far as the eye can see. It must go down to at least seventy-five to one hundred feet and even deeper in some spots. The trees are bare in the bottom from years of digging and removal of topsoil and coal. The stark branches bending with the wind. Feel the cold breeze blowing along the open ground. No matter when you are in the stadium even until today, the air is at least ten degrees colder or seems to be all over that area. Perhaps this is due to the exposure of the north and west sides or maybe it's something else.

Over the years this area saw its share of sorrow. Some people claim even today when you are there and it is quiet, you can make out the sounds of loneliness, the extra cold spots outside the stadium grounds. At least two suicides occurred in this area along with the discovery of an infant corpse. One of these suicides was extremely tragic in that the gentleman took a jar of dynamite, walked down into the pit and entered a shanty. He placed the jar under a board and laid his head upon it then lit the fuse. It was a horrible ending, but did it really stop there? An encounter over thirty years later may lead one to believe otherwise.

The winters in Summit Hill can be especially harsh as the town rests at an elevation that makes it snowier and harsher than the other towns in the Panther Valley. When it snows in Summit Hill, it can be brutally windy and bone chilling. It was during one of these snowstorms that a patrolman had a strange experience that he never forgot. It was an evening in January 1978 and a snowstorm gripped the area. He was making the rounds to be sure everyone was safe and no one was stranded in what was expected to be a decent storm.

Road near into former pit area west of the Ginter Stadium
(Photo by author)

As he was driving near the Ginter stadium he came across a hooded figure walking toward the quarry pit. He yelled to the figure to stop and it did. The police officer asked him who he was and why he was heading into the pit on such a nasty night. The figure simply said, "I'm Phil McCullough" and turned around and disappeared into wind driven snow as the darkened outline entered the stripping pit. At the time, the officer did not think much about it because a few of the local men had little shacks built in the woods where they went to hide from life mostly to drink.

He finished the night with no further incidents. When the chief came in for his shift the next morning, the patrolman related his encounter with the man. The chief was puzzled. "Who did you say you saw?" The patrolman repeated the figure's claim.

The older officer then said, "But it couldn't have been him. He died years ago by blowing himself up in the pit." The younger officer was stunned. Who did he really see that night? A person playing a joke on him or the shadow of a despondent man doomed to repeat his last act in the harsh winter night?

Postscript

Phil McCullough is buried in the GAR Cemetery in Summit Hill. I found his grave directly behind the office. According to a *Morning Call* newspaper article,[14] McCullough was found dead in the stripping pit near where the officer claimed to meet the ghostly figure. The authorities at that time ruled the death a suicide by dynamite explosion and stated another unexploded stick and blasting cap were near the body. The death certificate states he died on April 18, 1952 and the official ruling was "compound fracture of skull due to explosion."[15] He was buried on April 21, 1952 in the cemetery.

Contemporaries of the McCullough family remembered him as an unusual fellow, but none were able to shed any more information on what may have caused Mr. McCullough's demise although anecdotal evidence seems to support it may have been some family problems.

The Night that Sealed Campbell's Fate

The icy wind blew over Railroad Street (now Ludlow Street) in Summit Hill the night of December 2nd, 1871 as the day wound down for Morgan Powell, a mine boss in Summit Hill. He was briskly walking east as he did most days to the company store perhaps to pick up some supplies and catch up on local chatter before cutting across the railroad yard to his home on West Holland Street.

Former LCN Company Store and site of Morgan Powell shooting. Assassins alleged came from the visible side of building to shoot Powell in front of the store. (Photo by author)

As he neared the store, two masked assailants jumped out of the shadows of the building and confronted Powell, shot him at close range in the chest then turned and fled west down Railroad Street and into the stripping pit just beyond. Powell crumpled to the ground after the attack unable to move on his own.

Inside the store which was later known as McFadden's when I was growing up, the storekeeper and a few other unidentified men were socializing perhaps having a drink before heading home to their families that night. As they talked, possibly discussing their experiences of the day, they heard two muffled bangs that stopped the chatting. One ran to the door to see what happened and noticed the man laying near the storefront. Instinctively he looked down the street to see two men running in the distance.

Yelling for help, the other men came out of the store and helped bring the fallen man into the business and laid him on a table. When they saw the man was Powell, they immediately went for the Coal and Iron police. The police and a doctor arrived but to no avail. The doctor reported that Powell's wounds were mortal. Powell apparently was conscious but very weak. All the doctor could do was suggest they take him home and make him comfortable.

They carried him across the railroad yard to his home and got him comfortable in bed and waited. The police tried to get a statement, but Powell was unable to write although he supposedly told the officer he was attacked by a pair of masked men. The next day the officer returned with a written statement that identified two local Irishmen, Thomas Fisher and Lansford hotel owner Alexander Campbell, as his assassins. Powell was too weak at that point to sign anything so the officer took his hand and made a "X" on the document himself indicating Powell's supposed agreement with the statement.

Alexander Campbell

73

Powell died a day and a half later on December 4, 1871 and was buried in the local Presbyterian cemetery where his monument remains today. It is one of three remaining stones in that location which is now Memorial Park in Summit Hill.

No one to this day knows for sure who the murderers were that took the life of Powell, but it became the rope of the hangman's noose for Alexander Campbell who was implicated as a ringleader in the terroristic group known as the Molly Maguires. That statement intertwined the two men together in history forever.

Campbell was a tavern owner who emigrated to the United States in 1868 and set up shop eventually in the Storm Hill area of Lansford.[16] He became an officer in the Ancient Order of Hibernians, an Irish-American organization. The Irish were persecuted and discriminated against in the late 1800s in the mines which is what many believe led to the formation of the Mollies hidden within the AOH and their subsequent reign of terror in the coal regions of Carbon and Schuylkill counties.

James McParland aka James McKenna

In the same time period Philadelphia and Reading Railroad President Franklin Gowen was ruthlessly maneuvering a takeover of the anthracite coal mines in eastern Pennsylvania.[17] He hired the Pinkerton Detective Agency to help cement his control of the mines in the early 1870s. They sent one of their best men James McParland to infiltrate and gather information to end the opposition to his takeover in eastern Pennsylvania. McParland went undercover as James McKenna to supposedly gather evidence of the violence and terroristic acts that began occurring around the same time Gowen was making his move.

Proponents of the Mollies believe that McKenna played a part in these activities himself until his cover was blown. At that time Gowen had also managed to become the District Attorney in Schuylkill county and the two began the trials that resulted in men being hanged in 1877 for many murders and violent crimes in the coal regions none of which were directly tied to them except through McParland's testimony.

Campbell was caught up in this circle by his involvement with men who murdered mine superintendent John P. Jones one morning in Lansford. When Campbell was originally arrested and tried it was for conspiring in Jones' murder. He was found guilty in one of the many trials that took place and sentenced to hang. His family and supporters were desperate to save his life so they campaigned all the way to the governor from clemency. The mining officials seeing what was happening, produced the statement supposedly from Powell which identified Campbell as his assailant and that sealed the tavern owner's fate.

He was hanged on June 21, 1877 during the "Day of the Rope" in the Carbon County Prison along with his alleged fellow assassin Thomas Fisher. Prior to that as Campbell was being led from his cell, he pushed his hand against the dusty wall and stated his handprint would remain forever as a sign of his innocence. To this day the handprint is still found in the cell in the old prison which is now a museum.

Whether Campbell was one of the assailants that cold December evening remains an enigma of time and space. On a tour I took when the Delaware and Lehigh National Heritage Corridor along with the Summit Hill Historical Society placed historical markers at these sites, the tour guide said there was documentation that Powell may have been murdered by an angry husband instead of the Campbell and Fisher. He described Powell as having had affairs with some of the miners' wives in town while their spouses toiled in the mines. I have found no documentary proof of this, but it is worth noting.

It is also worth noting that many believed for decades these trials were unconstitutional kangaroo courts and the results of witch hunts motivated by Gowen's ruthless activities. The men were tried in court by attorneys paid for by the coal company with a jury selected by the coal company and comprised mostly of German and Pennsylvania Dutch immigrants who had a hard time understanding English and following the trial. On a personal note, my great-

great grandfather Daniel Remaley may have been one of those jurors. The defense attorneys were also Coal Company employees as well.

In 2005 and 2006, the Pennsylvania legislature passed resolutions asserting that the trials of these men were unconstitutional, and that the governor should do the same, but Governor Ed Rendell never recognized the resolutions.

This whole black episode in our local history is considered one of the earliest successful attempts at squashing an organized labor movement. It was events like these which in later years paved the way for unions to be established to protect future workers from similar miscarriages of justice. The fate of these men that persecuted the Mollys though may make people wonder about karma in that several of them later met mysterious and tragic deaths either at their own hands or the hands of another.

There is a final note to this story. Local legend has it that the cherub in the center of the park in Summit Hill is located at the spot where Powell collapsed in the railroad yard all those years ago on that cold December evening. It is said that on nights when it is still in the early winter, one can almost hear the gunfire and feel the presence of Campbell in the park. In fact, supposedly if you listen carefully you can hear a groan emanate from near the cherub; the groan of a dying man.

Postscript

The railroad yard was sold to the Borough of Summit Hill in the early 1900s to be used as a park. The park was named Ludlow Memorial Park after Lehigh Coal and Navigation President Edwin Ludlow who was heavily involved in the Summit Hill operation and helped organize and provide the land for the park for the town. Railroad Street's name was changed to honor Ludlow and the park was named after him. The park has become home to veteran's memorials from the Civil War to present day conflicts remembering Summit Hill's brave sons and daughters who gave their lives for our country. It is at the west end of this park where the memorial for Ginder's coal discovery stands as well.

Both James Gowen and James McParland did not escape their involvement unscathed. Gowen was found dead of a gunshot wound to the head in a room at the Wormley Hotel in Washington DC on December 13, 1889. [18]   While many initially attributed it to retribution by the Molly Maguires, it was quickly determined the turn in Gowen's business success in later years may have been the ultimate cause. He was ousted from the railroad and then engaged in a series of legal battles. His friends noticed his overall demeanor changed in 1889 and prior to heading to Washington DC to testify for a commerce hearing, he purchased a gun in a hardware store in Philadelphia which apparently was the instrument used in his death.[19]

McParland moved to Colorado where he continued to work for the Pinkerton Detective Agency and after uncovering fraud implicating the head of the office, he took over control. He continued to deal with union infiltration and investigations. His most famous case in later years was known as the Harry Orchard case in which Orchard aka Tom Hogan aka Albert Horsley assassinated Idaho Governor Frank Steunenberg. In later years, he was scarred with accusations of conspiring to commit voter fraud, jury tampering and lying under oath about the extent of his involvement in Molly Maguire activities. He died on May 18, 1919.[20]

The Dedicated Volunteers of Summit Hill

Original Summit Hill Armory photograph taken in late 1890's.
(Photo courtesy of Lee Mantz Estate Postcard Collection)

In the center of the town proper facing Ludlow Park almost directly across from where the Soldier's Monument is located stands the current Borough Fire Department and Community Center. This is the third building to occupy this property. During the 1800's when the mining industry was at its peak, the Lehigh Coal and Navigation Company commissioned and built an armory at this location to help maintain order in the borough and surrounding area. It housed a National Guard detachment and served for a time as the town's jail. In the early 1900s, the Armory burned and the stones that created it were removed and used to build other buildings in the area. In 1920, the town erected a borough hall on the site. This new hall housed the Fire Department, Water Authority, Police Department and the Borough office and garage.

The first floor of the building contained the fire department on the left, and the borough offices on the right. The Water Authority was in the front of the right first floor and had an entrance to the street. To the left of this office was a door that led to a hallway which winded through the downstairs. The borough office was midway down the hall and at the end of it was the entrance to the borough garage. Near the office door if one stayed left, there was a stairwell that led to the Police Department in the front second floor with the Council chambers occupying the second-floor rear. According to the people who worked and volunteered here, there was more here than meets the eye.

Police officers who worked in the office late at night described footfalls on the steps, yet no one ever appeared on the landing. Noises emanated from within the Council chamber with no known origin. Some officers speculated the sounds may have been prisoners from the original armory jail. In addition to the nightly noises, a couple patrolmen described the tiles in the suspended ceiling moving by themselves. Unlike a wind which would lift all of them simultaneously, a few officers claimed that the tiles lifted consecutively moving across the room like piano keys being pressed by a pianist running his fingers along the keyboard.

The left side of this building is where the Summit Hill Diligence Fire Department was located. The truck bays were in the front of the building with their large bay doors facing the Park. On the left side of the building were two side doors—one in the front of the building near the bay doors and the second midway down the building near the fire department meeting room. At one time the back room was open, but several years ago the volunteers decided to renovate the room converting it into a smaller meeting room, a kitchen and a loft above it for socializing.

Like many departments, Summit Hill's fire company is an all-volunteer organization of dedicated men and women who are tireless in their efforts to keep the town safe. It was not unusual to hear of volunteers who served forty or fifty plus years in the department. Some of the present volunteers claim that the former volunteers still return to pitch in and help with chores. When not on emergency calls, the men enjoyed spending time in the evenings in the social room at the station watching television, talking about sports and fraternizing together. The younger volunteers tended to use the meeting room and lounge as a gathering place in the spent many evenings there sometimes quite late into the night. Many times they would hear the door on the side open and slam shut due to the piston that kept the doors closed. They would hear the footfalls of someone in the garage heading toward the rear area yet as they waited no one would appear in the doorway. Newer volunteers would fruitlessly search the bay to see who was there without success.

One evening soon after the garage was renovated, a couple of the men were coming downstairs late at night. Off in the corner of the room opposite of the stairs, they noticed some movement in the low light. A soda machine had stood in the location of the activity, but it was moved when the room was renovated. As the men watched and their eyes became adjusted, they saw a figure stooped over at the wall. The figure turned and walked back to the side of the room and then returned a second time and knelt near the wall. As they watched, the man stood and turned toward them in the low light and then dissolved into the shadows. When they described the apparition to some other volunteers, they learned their night visitor was a deceased volunteer who was responsible for stocking the soda machine for the department.

In the early 2000's the borough acquired the neighboring St. Joseph's School Building and moved the police department and Borough office there. As some of the police officers worked alone in the building at night they reported hearing footsteps in the hallway and doors opening and closing. With the permission of the mayor and chief of police, some investigators were allowed to examine the building one evening, and while inside they also were a witness to the footfalls on the front stairs and in the upstairs area. Some unusual temperature readings and magnetic anomalies were recorded along with some interesting photographs.

For a period of three years before the building was torn down, the gym area was leased to a local wrestling promotion who trained there. The athletes reported several times seeing a nun standing sternly in one of the dark corners of the balcony. She would be there a few seconds and then vanish. Many times they felt like they were being watched.

Why would ghosts appear in a school? Some investigators theorize that when a person dies, they sometimes return to a place of comfort such as their childhood home or a haven. Others believe that a ghost can be drawn to a site of heavy trauma to try and find an answer or a reason. Another theory is that some ghosts travel through the area and are constantly passing through places. The explanation might be one or more of these theories or none of them at all. What is known is that if you stop, look and listen, they are all around us in places you may never expect.

Postscript

In 2005 the Summit Hill Borough Council began planning to renovate and build a new facility for the municipal offices. As part of this planning, they acquired the neighboring store that was to the east of the Borough Building. In 2008, demolition was started on all three properties. For the most part, there were no issues demolishing the store and the borough hall, but when it came to the school, the demolition crew reported several mechanical failures and problems that delayed tearing down the school. Some of the more superstitious people believed that the unearthly inhabitants of the school may have been trying to protect the building. Today a community center and new Fire Department stands on the parcel. The Borough offices, police department and Water Authority are located on Amidon Street.

Dance Hall Days

Like most of the industrious towns in northeastern Pennsylvania, Summit Hill was no stranger to recreation. The town had several taverns and hotels, a movie theater when movies became popular, pool halls and a dance hall named Park Hall. The two-story dance hall building was near the center of town right behind the Switchback Station between Ludlow Street and Holland Street. During its heyday, the hall was used not only for dancing, but local basketball games and semi-professional boxing matches also. It was a town social center from in the early twentieth century. It was converted into an apartment building in the mid-1940's as the semi-professional sports interest and social gatherings to dance began to wane.

People would come from all the area towns not just Summit Hill to attend events at Park Hall. It is said that more than a few young men and ladies met their future spouses at this hall. The young adults that traveled to town from Lansford would either walk along the highway or use one of several paths that wound around the treacherously deep stripping pits. One of these "land bridges" was located on the eastern side of town near where the Little League field can be found today. Besides being used by young people, the bridge was used by miners traveling down to work in the Number 6 mine near Andrewsville. Unfortunately, it was also used by robbers and thugs who would mug the miners heading home on payday. Several men are alleged to have been robbed and some murdered on these remote paths.

Young adults using this land bridge east of town would tell hushed stories about strange experiences on these paths especially at night, and only a brave few would walk this bridge alone after sunset. Many of them reported feeling like they were being watched. One of the more intense experiences some reported was a column of ectoplasm that appeared near this bridge and followed those traveling on this bridge area before dissipating. This ectoplasm not only was a visual phenomenon, but a physical one as well. It usually had a nauseating stench that reportedly nauseated the walkers when it appeared. This supernatural harassment continued and intensified until finally an Episcopal priest was persuaded to bless the land. It is said that he spent three days near the bridge blessing it and returned spiritually drained and exhausted but satisfied that he was able to dispel the presence.

The bridge wasn't the only source of danger. Unsuspecting souls traveling other wooded paths in the area were easy targets for muggings so many tried their best not to walk alone. One evening some young ladies were heading to the dance hall and had walked up one of the better-traveled paths from Lansford to Summit Hill. Deciding to save some time, they cut through a few of the cemeteries on the eastern edge of the town instead of taking the long way down and across town. This shortcut would cut five or ten minutes off their walk. As they headed through the cemeteries, they saw a man ahead of them. He was sitting on top of a tombstone near the edge of a cemetery watching them as they closed in on his location.

When they were near enough, he motioned to them to come close to him. They noticed he was dressed in eveningwear, a dress suit that most miners could not afford and probably would not wear except to funerals or church. He seemed odd to the ladies, but he spoke quietly and firmly to them. "Go back down into town to walk to the hall. Do not continue on this path as there is trouble ahead."

This older stranger did not scare them, but their anxiety increased due to his insistent tones and his unusual directions. They decided to forgo the shortcut through the cemetery and took the longer path through the northern part of town. When the ladies had walked a short distance away, they paused and decided to turn and thank him, but when they looked back to where he was perched on the stone, he was gone. Nervously, the girls scampered toward the haven of the borough streets.

Later that evening, the girls learned how the stranger may have saved them. Sometime later that evening, a few men walking the path took the shortcut the girls had originally planned to use. Hidden among the stones in the cemetery was a bandit with a knife. The young men were attacked but they were able to overpower this brigand and after subduing him, they dragged him into town to the constable. If the girls had continued walking on their original path, they could have gotten seriously hurt or worse. No one ever learned the identity of this guardian angel who these girls encountered that fateful night, and he was never seen in the area again.

Postscript

Many towns had dance halls of various sizes that served as gathering places for people in the late nineteenth century and the first half of the twentieth century. They would have live bands and dancing to provide a social hub for folks in the area as well as sporting events. Unfortunately, other than notices about public events and social affairs being held at the Hall were the only items found when researching in local papers.

With regard to the story about the path, it should be noted that sometimes tales like this were told to keep young people from straying into unsafe areas alone, but there is probably many kernels of truth in this story. Highwaymen and bandits were not unheard of along the desolated roads and paths throughout the coal regions. The police presence was rather limited making such activities for these brigands enticing. There was a story I found at one point in the Valley Gazette archive that discussed an unnamed stranger who was visiting one of Summit Hill's numerous bars in the late 1800's. As he drank that evening, he became inebriated and talkative showing the local miners his small cache of gold coins. The next morning, his battered body was found at the edge of town near a path heading toward Lansford. While the Coal and Iron police ruled the death accidental due to misadventure, the article noted that none of the gold coins were ever found.

A Roadside Encounter

Summit Hill has its own share of tragic accidents on the mountainous roads within the borough limits. One well-known accident occurred when a young woman's car left the highway and traveled into the woods killing her almost instantly. Another woman was murdered in the Inn that once stood on Bugzie's Mountain—strangled it is said by her jealous husband. There was a third on Lentz Trail in which a jealous boyfriend in a car pursued his girlfriend as they sped down the road. He eventually caused her to lose control and crash resulting in her death.

Over the years, people have claimed to see women in white dresses wandering along the roads near the scenes of these accidents. One man in the early pre-dawn hours on his way to work was startled to see a woman in a white gown come out of the woods to the side of the road barefooted and tried to wave him down. He passed her not comprehending what he saw initially. As he realized that this was someone who may need help, he slowed down and looked in the rear-view mirror, but there was no one on the road any longer.

One evening an area resident reported to me along with a convenience store clerk to whom he spoke of another unnerving encounter. It was a rainy, foggy evening in the fall. It was already dark as he reported having headlights on as he navigated down Bugzie's Mountain. Somewhere between there and Summit Hill proper, his headlights caught hazy image of a woman in the dense fog on the road. He braked hard, but as the car skidded to a stop, the woman passed through the hood and the passenger compartment disappearing as it existed out the back of the vehicle. The man was frightened and instinctively hit the gas and sped into town stopping at the convenience store, as he said it was the first place that had people. The clerk reported him coming in out of breath and relating the story to her.

A friend of mine who worked the late shift also reported seeing a woman in white on the same mountain as he was heading home. His sighting described her as a young woman in a long white gown.

Postscript

The white lady stories are universal both in description and in situation. Late at night a woman dressed in a white dress or a gown appears near the side of the road motioning for help. A driver stops to help her, and she gets into the car and tells him where she needs to go. He drives her to that destination and when he turns to let her out, she is gone. In some cases, she is cold so he offers a topcoat to her to wear. Usually he learns that she was not of this earth because her destination is typically a person's home. Upon arriving, the driver is shocked to find that the young lady had been tragically killed in a car accident near the spot where the driver picked her up. Upon further investigation at the local cemetery, the man finds his coat folded up on the ground/draped over the gravestone or something similar. This urban legend has been told countless times with the most famous case being that of "Resurrection Mary" near Chicago.

The Stranded Hunters

My friend Steve tells a strange tale from his teens when he was hunting on the southwest side of the mountain many years ago. He and a companion were hunting during the first week of buck season which in Pennsylvania would be the end of November. They were on the southwest side of the mountain toward Tamaqua. They spent most of the afternoon in the woods, but they knew a storm was coming, although they figured they had a few more hours of light before the evening snowstorm started. Unfortunately, they were caught by surprise as the sky started to darken much earlier than they anticipated. Before they could make it along the path to the road, the storm arrived, and it was snowing heavily within minutes of its onset. The early storm caused darkness to envelope the woods much sooner. They wandered in the direction of the road for at least an hour before they realized in the dark that they were lost. The storm was expected to last several hours so they tried to find a covered area to wait out the foul weather. They found a protected spot under some bushes to wait out the storm when they heard a noise.

Up ahead was a figure motioning to them. The boys went toward the figure who was holding a lantern. It was a man in his forties.

He said, "Are you boys lost?"

They told him they were. He invited them to follow him and he would help them. They figured that the both of them would be okay if he tried anything sinister, so they consented to follow him. He led them for several minutes into the forest and up ahead they could see some lights and smoke rising out of the chimney of a small hunting cabin.

"You boys will be okay here for a bit. You can warm up and have some water, and if you'd like, I will take you back to the road," he said.

Tentatively, the boys thanked him and followed him inside.

Inside the single room dwelling they found a second man wearing an oversized red plaid hunting jacket and hat. The man that had led them to the cabin was also wearing a quite unusual coat in that it was one that was not in style and had not been for several years. The men made small talk with the boys and my friend said that the one thing that was odd to him was that the men mispronounced many local names including the town of Tamaqua. Several years ago, it was pronounced more the way local Indians talked rather than the way we do now. That struck my friend as quite odd. The teens stayed and talked to the two strange but friendly men. Finally the first man asked if they wanted to stay longer or get back to the road.

Knowing how late it was getting and not wanting to worry anyone, the boys decided to return to town. The first man got dressed and when the boys were ready, he led them out of the cabin back into the woods. After about fifteen minutes, they arrived at the road. Along their travel, my friend paid attention to landmarks so that they could find the cabin in the future. When they reached the road, he asked if he could be of any further assistance. The boys said that they would be okay, so at that point they parted ways. My friend told me that he turned to say something to the man but that fast he was gone.

Fortunately, the boys made it home safely. The next spring my friend and his friend decided to go back to that area and find the cabin and maybe the men to thank them. He retraced what he determined was their steps—first along the road and then into the woods down the rise to where the cabin should be, but nothing was there. At that point the boys began a general search of the area, yet there was no cabin anywhere close by. To this day, my friend will tell you that he is certain he was in the right place and was totally stumped. Perhaps the cabin did exist and my friend just got lost in the winter storm. Maybe the men will recognize themselves and let me know so that my friend can thank them. Or just maybe, the cabin was a home housed by angels that protected my friend and his friend and kept them safe from a howling winter storm.

Postscript

The valley between Summit Hill and Bugzie's Mountain, as well as the thousands of acres of undeveloped ground on the sides of both mountains is prime hunting ground in the area. When we were teens, many of us would hunt with our fathers in the White Bear Valley. I spent several mornings and evenings with my father rabbit hunting and deer hunting as a teen. My friends would sometimes go on their own. Today there are several homes down in the valley along the Owl Creek Road, but thirty years ago, homes in this valley were quite remote with most being erected near the main roads and at least thousands of feet apart from each other. From Summit Hill to Route 309 and Jim Thorpe, much of the valley except for a few farms was pristine woodland. Even today most of the mountainsides are still undeveloped due to their steep slopes. It is on the side of this mountain where a friend of mine spent a strange evening.

Along these paths in the woods area men used to build hunting cabins. These cabins were quite simple buildings and more like sheds than an actual cabin. Some of the larger landowners would have several cabins in the woods that they used during hunting season. Even in the early part of this century, it wasn't unusual to find cabins in the woods. Unlike today, many of these buildings were respected and used but not damaged. I grew up in the 1970s and 1980s and by that time, there weren't many cabins left in the woods and those that remained were mostly rundown and abandoned.

Swinging Doors and The Phantom Singer

Summit Hill Heritage Center, Former St. Paul's United Church of Christ.
(Photo by the author)

I grew up going to St. Paul's United Church of Christ on the corner of Hazard and Chestnut Streets in town. My grandfather, both of my parents and many of the people I knew growing up served on council there. My forebears were one of the families that helped build the church. The people were leased a tract of land from the Lehigh Coal and Navigation Company for one dollar with the understanding it was to be used for a church. In 1865, the original sanctuary was constructed with its entrance in the bell tower on the corner. In the early 1900's, the building was remodeled and expanded. The entrance was moved to the center of the Chestnut street side onto the expansion. About twenty or thirty years later, Sunday school rooms were added to the rear of the building and the basement was dug out so that a dining hall and kitchen could be added. My grandfather told me he and most of the men did this.

Unfortunately, a passionate disagreement over a new pastor led to a massive schism in the church in the late 1980's and on October 14, 2007, the doors closed, but my cousin Lyle Mantz and his wife Andrea who were the leaders on council wanted to see the building live on in a new way. In the final years before the closure, the church gave the Summit Hill Food Pantry a place to locate by providing space in the basement. With the church closing, they wanted to maintain this home. Through much negotiation with the Penn Northeast Synod and the help of volunteers including me, we reopened the building as the Summit Hill Heritage Center on October 1, 2009 and it has been functioning as a non-profit organization and charity hosting events, renting the hall for parties and continuing to maintain the food pantry and other community services.

Soon after the Heritage Center opened its doors to provide this new mission however, some interesting things began to occur. We would be sitting in the social hall section of the building where we would meet and hold events in the evenings. The sanctuary would be dark and shadowed. We could plainly see into the massive hall with its high arched ceilings through three large open arched windows that separated the two rooms. These windows originally had pull-down covers that could be used to isolate the sanctuary from these large multi-purpose rooms in the expansion. Their purpose was to provide overflow seating for the sanctuary. As we sat there, many of us observed shadow figures moving up and down the main aisle in the sanctuary. Their appearance was unpredictable and sporadic, but they were seen on several occasions.

Our mail is delivered through the small outside door at the rear of the building in what was the sacristy. Volunteers would retrieve it from the box we placed under the door slot. One day one of our volunteers was exiting the sacristy into the sanctuary when she saw the massive, heavy oak swinging door open at the rear of the church and then swing closed. This door was the egress to the narthex. There was no one there as evidenced by the fact that the big windows in the door revealed no one. This startled her and she quickly left the sanctuary through a side door that connected to the expansion near the old church office.

Others witnessed this as well. I happened to talk with a childhood friend about this strange report and he caught me by surprise. He said, "You know, I never told anyone this, but that happened a long time ago when we were kids too. I [with another friend] was sitting on the steps in the narthex and the doors to the Sunday School swung open towards us by themselves. We jumped to our feet to see who it was, but there was no one there."

We asked the Blue Mountain Paranormal Society to investigate the building for us in 2013. As part of the preliminary investigation, one of the crew set a tape recorder in the Sunday School room. As they checked the building out and interviewed us, the recorder was left running in the empty room. Later they retrieved it and upon playback, a woman could be heard singing "In the Garden" on the recording. It was only then I learned that a woman named Gladys used to sing that song as a solo in the choir and in Sunday School. Several times after that during impromptu investigations, we would play the piano and her melodious voice would occasionally be heard over the notes from the piano.

On occasion, I would play the old pipe organ (not very well) when the building was empty. One evening as I played while waiting for a lecturer to arrive, I saw blue streaks of energy crossing back and forth above me in the high arches of the sanctuary. I was amazed, but when I stopped playing they disappeared. When I told our President Deb about this, she told me on more than one occasion she would be sitting in one of the rear Sunday School rooms which we converted to an office and would hear the organ playing. She came out to see who it was but as she entered the main room, the music would stop: the organ was off. After that encounter, she no longer bothered to check on the phantom organist.

One hot July evening prior to a show we were going to have featuring celebrity impersonators, we decided because of the nature of the performance and the makeup needed by the performers to move it to the air-conditioned borough community center. The church did not have air conditioning at the time. The community center did not have a stage, but we had a sectional stage that was portable. It was stored in the "dungeon room" in the rear of the basement where the oil tanks were kept. A few of the men including my cousin Lyle decided to retrieve them and set them up in the community center for the show. One of the men, Peter[21] headed to the Center to dig them out. As he worked in the rear of the basement alone and waiting for Lyle, he heard the door open and footsteps enter the building and come down the basement stairs. He left the dungeon and walked down the hall to greet the assistants who had arrived to move the stage with him in the dining hall, but as he turned the corner, there was no one there. Lyle and his helpers arrived a few minutes later to find Peter shaken up sitting in the dining hall. After that evening, he refused to be in the basement alone.

It was in this building though that I had my own paranormal encounter and it was the third time I saw a full-bodied apparition. The unique thing about this for me though was this apparition appeared in broad daylight. It was January 2014, and it was a bitter cold Sunday morning. We were having issues with the oil burner running and someone had to manually turn it on prior to events. That afternoon there was a hall rental so we wanted to make sure the heat was running. Deb called me to go up and check everything. I got out of bed and went to the building about 9AM. It was sunny but cold. I went inside and locked the door behind me to make sure no one followed me inside. After I went down to the basement and turned on the oil burner, talking to the building as I went just out of habit partially and partially to not feel alone, I returned to the narthex. I decided since I was there just to do a walk through to verify the building was empty.

I went up the left set of stairs and through the massive oak doors into the Sunday school area multi-purpose rooms. The light from the beautiful stained-glass windows here and the massive ones in the sanctuary flooded the open space but because of how large these rooms were, the center of the Sunday school was still slightly shadowed. I went left and walked into the connected back rooms verifying everything was secured. I followed the path I took back to the Sunday School rooms as the door on the furthest small room that would have exited by the old church office was locked. I walked back to the massive oak doors. From where I was standing, I could easily see the brightly sunlit sanctuary and the side entrance to it from the church office through an open alcove there. I called Deb to tell her everything was secure and running properly.

As she answered the phone, I saw a full figure in a long black robe with a hooded head walk out of the church office and into the side door of the sanctuary and promptly disappear as it passed through that doorway. I said, "I

93

will call you back," and hung up on her as I ran toward the alcove. There was no one there, no one in the office room and no one at all in the sanctuary. I called her back and told her why I hung up on her. It was amazing and yet not scary. I believe I just witnessed a time slip or an environmental memory. The interesting thing was the apparition was solid and looked normal, but it simply vanished into the light in the sanctuary. To date, I have not seen the figure again.

Postscript

The Summit Hill Heritage Center is a non-profit organization that houses several tenants at this point. The main mission is to continue operating a food pantry for Summit Hill Residents. Early 2020, the Summit Hill Historical Society decided to rent space in the building from the Heritage Center so they spent the first half of 2020 moving the museum from its location in the old company store[22] to the building. The Church on the Rock also rents the sanctuary weekly for services. They look forward to building a pavilion on the lot donated to them by an anonymous benefactor which is across the alley from the building and the former site of the Episcopal Church.

In fact these two sites along with the Italian American Club (the former Baptist Church) and the Hope of Christ Presbyterian Church formed the four corners of the block referred to as "Holy Square". Supposedly this block was featured in one of the columns written by famed journalist and chronicler of the weird Robert Ripley. The column "Ripley's Believe It or Not" was a widely syndicated feature in most local newspapers. As of this time, I have not been able to locate this column or cartoon to substantiate the claim.

BONUS SHORT STORY: Edmund Brennan And The Eagle Hotel

(Note: This ghost story was used on the first year of the Summit Hill ghost tour as a "trick" for people to see if they could find the story that wasn't true. It could have been, but it wasn't. To spell it out, enjoy the following work of fictional terror.)

The Real Eagle Hotel in Summit Hill
(Photograph Courtesy of Lee Mantz Estate Postcard Collection)

Edmund Brennan was an ox of a man with a brilliant head of red hair and a fiery Irish temper to match. Rumor had it that he came to the United States to avoid murder charges in Ireland. Apparently a fellow Irishman made the mistake of wooing a young lady Edmund had eyes on, so Edmund set him

95

straight—straight into a solid oak table head first causing the young man's premature demise. None of it was substantiated, but rumors circulated by people trying to explain who this man was. He quickly got a job in the mines as a hard worker and one not afraid to freely carry large amounts of black powder, a substance necessary to knock the coal loose. In addition, he always had a small pick-axe attached to his belt just over his right hip.

Edmund was alone for the first few months he had moved to Summit Hill, but one night on his way home from work, he met Molly, a pretty, young barmaid who helped to wait on customers in the bar. He quickly became infatuated with her and tried to win her affections. Molly appreciated the attention, but just did not share the same level of interest in Edmund, although she flirted with him anyway. One evening a shipping executive named Thomas Coleman arrived in town to meet with Morgan Powell about some mining contracts. He checked into the hotel and quickly met and became attracted to Molly. He asked her after work to come up to his room and share a nightcap. Molly agreed, telling Thomas that her shift would be ending in about a half hour. Thomas retired to his room leaving a key for Molly at his table. She cleaned up the table and put it in her pocket.

At that point, Edmund came into the bar. He was tired so he asked the bartender for some ale to go and provided him with his canteen from work. As the bartender filled it, Edmund greeted Molly and asked her about her day. She told him it was uneventful and that she was tired. He asked if she had long to work and she told him she would be done soon. When she was finished, she planned to go home to bed. Edmund wished her a good night and paid the bartender for the ale, then left the hotel. When the shift ended, she slipped upstairs to Thomas' room, taking the stairs so she would not be noticed. It was also possible to get to the second floor on the outside by going up the steps from the street to the wraparound porch on the second story of the building, but Molly wanted to be discreet.

Soon after she went upstairs, Edmund returned to the bar to give her a piece of fool's gold that he had found near the mine during the day. Fool's Gold, also known as iron pyrite, is a substance that sparkles like gold and is found near areas where coal is mined. He had forgotten to give it to her before he left the hotel so he returned hoping to catch her before she went home. He looked around the bar for her to no avail. As he was leaving, he supposedly heard two men talking about the scoundrel from the shipping company and his attempt to cut into the mining business. The other man mentioned he couldn't wait to get steal from Powell; he was already stealing Molly's favors. He mentioned to his bar mate seeing Colby leave the key on the table and Molly slipping it into her dress.

Edmund lost all control at this point. He was enraged to believe another man could possibly be getting the attention of his girl, the love of his life. His rage became consuming and violent. He stormed out of the bar and quickly found the staircase leading up to the second story porch. As he sneaked from window to window trying to locate his Molly, someone on the street went to find the constable to report a prowler. Meanwhile, Edmund had located the young lovers and watched them until he could no longer contain his rage. As he burst into the room, the young lovers were semi-clothed in a tight embrace and kissing passionately. In one fluid motion, Edmund grabbed his trusty pick-axe, raised it over his head, and with one mighty swing, he brought it down cleaving Thomas' skull open. The force of the blow and Colby's skull flying forward caused Molly's nose to break as she flew back onto the bed screaming hysterically. Edmund had the lifeless lover by the back of his collar and shoved him onto the bed beside her. Next, he raised the axe again and brought it down into the young man's chest with such force that it separated the breastbone. Reaching into his chest, the homicidal Edmund yanked his heart out and shoved it into Molly's mouth to silence her. These events were pieced together from an examination of the room, but the next events were witnessed by dozens of people and the constable.

Edmund grabbed Molly off the bed smashing his hand into her face to keep the organ jammed in her mouth and dragged her out onto the balcony. Between the broken nose and subsequent abuse, it seemed to the witnesses that she was unconscious at this point. With a loud roar, he yanked up her limp body over his head in preparation to throw her from the porch. At the same time, the constable had made his way up to the porch and was just behind the corner with his pistol drawn. When he heard Edmund yell, he rounded the corner, raised his pistol and fired. The madman appeared to be unfazed by the bullet and tossed her to the street below where she struck her head on a curb and instantly died. Edmund turned on him and as the lunatic miner started to charge him, the constable opened fire again. This time the bullet found its mark in Edmund's skull right through the nose. The hulk of an Irishman immediately fell face forward onto the porch. He survived about fifteen minutes before succumbing to his mortal injuries.

The hotel cleaned up after the tragedy and tried to put the past behind them, but several times they had guests refuse to stay in the room where this incident took place. The help began to get used to people getting up in the middle night and demanding another room. When asked what the problem was, they said that they were woken by a loud crash followed by a feeling of something being thrown on the bed. When they opened their eyes, they saw a hulking shadow standing at the doorway onto the porch glaring into the room. All of them also noticed the crop of red hair on the top of his head. When they went to rise from the bed, the figure slowly dissolved right before their eyes. After a while, the hotel decided to convert the room and use it for storage.

One night after all the guests had turned in for the night, the owner was cleaning up the bar when he thought he smelled smoke. He headed for the roof and began to wake the guests. When he got to the second floor, the smoke got denser and a new smell mingled with the smoke a faint scent of black powder. By this time, guests were waking other guests and soon everyone was on the ground floor. The fire company was a few doors away and quickly responded to the conflagration, but try as they might, the fire stubbornly refused to extinguish and some onlookers said that it appeared that three people were still trapped in the second floor. The chief questioned the owner who told him that the reservations were light and everyone was standing nearby. Within minutes of this conversation, a powerful explosion blew apart the top of the hotel and brought it crashing down into the building. A second explosion on the second floor in the area of the converted hotel room brought the building down in a violent collapse. It was rumored that the smell of burning black powder permeated the area.

The cause of the fire was never determined, and the hotel was never rebuilt. The factory that occupies its location has operated several years without incident, but it is said that on certain nights of the year during the early spring, you can catch the scent of black powder riding on the night breeze.

Postscript

This story was written by me the first year we conducted a ghost tour in Summit Hill. At the time, I was an officer in the Summit Hill Historical Society in the late 1990's. I vacationed in Gettysburg, Pennsylvania and Williamsburg, Virginia and in both locations, I went on ghost tours. Taking a tour and learning the folklore of those towns fascinated me. It was a mixture of spookiness, legend and folklore that encouraged me to do the same here.

We were trying to open a museum and looking for funds to secure the space. I suggested to the group we run a ghost tour. They trusted me enough to give me the permission to start preparing one. I reached out to the community. My theory was that ghosts and urban legends go hand in hand with strong emotions and trauma—something of which the coal regions have no shortage.

When word circulated someone was looking for this type of story, the tales came flowing toward me. I interviewed local police and at least a dozen people. Once we had enough source material, the next step was figuring out how to promote it. We decided to have some fun in the process.

Instead of just listening, we wanted to give our guests a challenge, so I authored a tale based on one of the local landmarks. We kept it a secret and only I knew the story until the tour began.

The Eagle Hotel stood originally near the Armory in Summit Hill. It was torn down very early in the borough's history, but I thought it would make a great setting for this story and since we had no real legends surrounding it, this seemed a plausible backdrop for this short tale. Surprisingly, very few people knew this was the false story that first year. It was only ever used that first year; in subsequent tours, we stuck to stories that were documented and researched.

The tours lasted for four years before other area towns caught on to the idea and began holding their own versions. I conducted tours twice after that. In 2014, I did a ghost tour for the Heritage Center as a fundraiser that involved a cemetery storytelling followed by a ghost hunt at the Center. Last year was the first time we did a cemetery walking tour of the Grand Army Cemetery which was appropriate since many of the stories center around the property or people buried in it or close by.

About The Author

David Wargo has worn many hats over the years, but is most proud of being a paranormal investigator, local folklorist, historian and volunteer as well as a retired correspondent for the local Times News newspaper. As a correspondent he wrote over 600 columns and reported on local events for twelve years before retiring. His columns for the most part focused on magic and the paranormal. He had an article published in FATE magazine in 2004 relating ghost stories about the Grand Army Cemetery. As a historian, he is a past president of the Summit Hill Historical Society. For the last ten years he has been the President of the Board of Directors for the Grand Army of the Republic Cemetery in Summit Hill.

He is an active paranormal investigator for the last twenty five years. He was a founder of the Panther Valley Paranormal Society, member of the Blue Mountain Paranormal Society and board member of Paranormal Sightings of PA. In that capacity, he has researched and investigated many public and private cases throughout Pennsylvania, Maryland and New Jersey.

In addition, he previously co-wrote a manuscript Specters of Summit Hill and other smaller items for the Summit Hill Historical Society as well as some plays for churches he attended. He is also a retired part-time professional magician which aids in his paranormal investigations and has performed throughout Pennsylvania and in Maryland, Ohio and Vermont.

References

Kreamer, R. (1954, September 26). Style of Tombstones are Keeping Pace With Progress in Stonecutting Methods. *The Morning Call*, p. 21.

Ostlund, M. (2014). *Find'em, Chase'em, Sink'em.* Guilford, CT: Old Saybrook Lyon Press.

Williams, A. (2002, October). Death on the Nile. *National Geographic*, pp. 2-25.

Ostlund, M. (2014). Find 'em, Chase 'em, Sink 'em. Guilford, Connecticut: Old Saybrook Lyon Press.

Williams, A. (2002, October). Death on the Nile. National Geographic , pp. 2-25.

End Notes

[1] See *The Late Night Visitor* on page 16

[2] _____., The Shadowlands website. Link: http://theshadowlands.net/ghost/

[3] "Petrified Body", The Milwaukee Journal, February 24, 1903, p. 12. Link: http://news.google.com/newspapers?id=zHQxAAAAIBAJ&sjid=rCAEAAAAIBAJ&pg=3525%2C5091615

[4] "Summit Hill Still Pays Respects to Borough 'Unknown Soldier'", The Morning Call, Allentown, PA. May 29, 1961, p.5. Link: https://www.newspapers.com/image/275294081/?terms=Frederick%2BLeiber

[5] _____.,"First Unknown Soldier", Reading Eagle, June 12, 1927, p. 2. Link: http://news.google.com/newspapers?id=CJ4hAAAAIBAJ&sjid=1ZkFAAAAIBAJ&pg=2485%2C2268741

[6] Link: https://www.waltersmonument.com/about

[7] "Mary E. Bruzgo, Co-Owned Marble And Granite Company In Summit Hill", The Morning Call, Allentown, PA August 4, 1992, p. 24. Link: https://www.mcall.com/news/mc-xpm-1992-08-04-2873585-story.html

[8] _____., "Double Murder May Be Black Hand Work", Reading Eagle, September 8, 1911, p 15. Link: https://news.google.com/newspapers?id=VYotAAAAIBAJ&sjid=E5wFAAAAIBAJ&pg=3477%2C835421

[9] Mantz, Lee., "Images of America: Summit Hill"., Arcadia Publishing Co., Chicago, IL., 2009. p. 97.

[10] It was explained to me at one point by my cousin Lee Mantz that the road was named the Kitchen Road because it entered Summit Hill at the end of the town and not through the center as Pine Street or Chestnut Street connect the highway to the town. This is similar to the kitchen typically being in the back of a home.

[11] Kreamer, Ralph, "Pay Wagon Murders of 1911 Unsolved". The Morning Call, Allentown, PA., November 1, 1993. Link: http://articles.mcall.com/1993-11-01/news/2950280_1_samuel-watkins-lansford-payroll

[12] Kreamer, Ralph, "Hell's Kitchen Road Killing of 2 in 1911 Still Unsolved". The Morning Call, Allentown, PA April 3, 1955. P. 7.

[13] _____.,"Anniversary of Unsolved Double Murder". Mauch Chunk Times News, Mauch Chunk, PA September 7, 1943. P. 1 Link: https://www.newspapers.com/clip/58164746/anniversary-of-unsolved-double-murder/

[14] _____, "Dynamite Used By Miner, 60, To End Life". The Morning Call, Allentown, PA, April 19, 1952. Link: https://www.newspapers.com/clip/21580111/dynamite_used_by_miner_to_end_life

[15] Pennsylvania, Commonwealth of. 1952 (Filed 21 April). *Certificate of Death: Philip McCullough.* Dept. of Health, Bureau of Vital Statistics, Reg. Dist. No. 1365-146. File No. 32357. Informant: Clara McCullough [nee. Clara Yates], Summit Hill, PA.

[16] _____, "The Molly Maguires (1970)" Link: https://www.lehigh.edu/~ineng/paw/paw-history.htm

[17] "Execution of Molly Maguires Historical Marker." ExplorePAHistory.com, Pennsylvania Historical and Museum Commission, 2011, explorepahistory.com/hmarker.php?markerId=1-A-3B9.

[18] "Franklin B. Gowen." Wikipedia, Wikimedia Foundation, 7 July 2018, en.wikipedia.org/wiki/Franklin_B._Gowen.

[19] Ibid.

[20] "James McParland." Wikipedia, Wikimedia Foundation, 7 July 2018, en.wikipedia.org/wiki/James_McParland.

[21] Not his real name
[22] See *The Night That Sealed Campbell's Fate.*

Made in the USA
Middletown, DE
23 October 2020

22543505R10064